East African Childhood

Three Versions

edited by
Lorene K. Fox

written by
Joseph A. Lijembe
Anna Apoko
J. Mutuku Nzioki

Nairobi
OXFORD UNIVERSITY PRESS
Lusaka Addis Ababa London New York
1967

Oxford University Press, Ely House, London W. I.

GLASGOW NEW YORK TORONTO MELBOURNE WELLINGTON
CAPE TOWN SALISBURY IBADAN NAIROBI LUSAKA ADDIS ABABA
BOMBAY CALCUTTA MADRAS KARACHI LAHORE DACCA
KUALA LUMPUR HONG KONG TOKYO

Made and Printed in East Africa

Contents

THORNS IN THE GRASS: The Story of a Kamba Boy
by *J. Mutuku Nzioki*

Dedication

To the first Bachelor of Education Class
Makerere University College
Kampala, Uganda
1963—1966

Introduction

These three versions of *East African Childhood** were written originally, as were twenty-one others, to meet the requirements of a class in Human Learning and Development, the first course in the new three-year Bachelor of Education programme at Makerere University College, 1963-1966. Although the students were preparing for secondary school positions, it was felt important that they have a chance to consider human development from birth onwards.

The collection of child development and psychology references in the Education Library at Makerere was varied and extensive, mostly by Western authors, about Western children, and illustrated with only white faces. The students made good use of these books in the course, as well as of the very helpful but all too few research studies which colleagues and friends helped us to locate, about African and other non-Western children and youth. All these readings, Western and non-Western, we related where applicable to what we ourselves were observing and discovering about East African children, both in school and out. It was in part to augment the non-Western collection that the students were asked, as a major assignment, to study further and write about growing up in their own tribes, sixteen of which were represented in the class, along with one Asian community. The students' own learning, including more positive self-perception, was of course the primary concern.

At this point in their education these students had neither the skills nor the time to do extensive bona fide research. Rather they were encouraged to draw from their own recollections, from observations and discussions with their families and village elders, and from relevant readings where available, what they felt would frame an honest picture, and to write this up in whatever form they preferred. Such papers, I assured them in their modesty, organized and written 'from inside the tribe', could be valuable supplements to the more objective, long-term research studies we were using, carried on in the main by expatriate specialists in the social science fields.

---

* East Africa consists of Kenya, Uganda, and Tanzania (formerly Tanganyika and Zanzibar). Tanganyika became independent of the British in 1961, Uganda in 1962, Kenya and Zanzibar in late 1963.

The writing of the papers was a two-term assignment. This meant that the students could spend the one month holiday between terms in their villages, observing, checking, interviewing—in effect, looking anew at their family and tribal customs, especially as related to children and youth. Before the students left for their homes, I requested our Department (Educational Psychology) to provide film for those students who had cameras or access to cameras (about half the class), to secure photographs suitable for illustrating the papers. Hence, a related but quite unexpected consequence, suggested by the quality and scope of the pictures brought back, was a photographic exhibition at the new Uganda Museum. The exhibition, entitled 'Child Development in East Africa', consisted of about sixty or seventy large prints of selected photographs (some of which appear in these pages), for the whole community to view. Later the showing was repeated by request at the main Makerere College Library.

In addition to the informational contribution the photographs and the papers could make, I had several purposes in mind in setting up such assignments. Among the most important were: (1) to help the students see the ways of learning and growing up in their own tribes and communities as worthy of respect and study; (2) to help them become increasingly aware that their experiences and learning as young children have helped significantly to determine the kinds of persons they are now; (3) to get them to talk and write freely about themselves and the African traditions which have helped to shape them; (4) to help them view and deal with the children in their own environment, both at home and at school, in a more understanding and constructive way, drawing upon and simultaneously giving meaning and reality to their wide reading and to the class lectures and discussions; and (5) to help them see themselves as competent thinkers, talkers, writers—at this time when writing by Africans, about Africans, for Africans, was so urgently needed and requested. How the various ways of viewing and reviewing child development through such projects, supplemented by the more formal systematic study as called for in the course outline, would enable the students to be prepared for the forthcoming, all-important examination in this field, was also in my mind—and in theirs. Long-held faith in learning through thoughtful observation, wholehearted participation, and discovery, was later vindicated when every member of the class did pass what the external British examiner called a 'very difficult examination'.

By the end of the second term (and of my own extended leave from Queens College), the students' papers had been written, edited, titled, illustrated in some cases, and handed in to be bound for use in the Education Library. I returned to New York at the time with several of the papers, selected mainly in terms of the scope of the problems they dealt with, and their varied approach and style. Stopping in Nairobi, Kenya, en route, I showed the papers (and the photographs) to Oxford University Press, who expressed interest, provided I could help the students get them ready for publication.

From June to September of 1965, I was back in East Africa for this very purpose. And an exciting though time-consuming task it was, to be sure. By this time the students were beginning the first term of their final year. Although their free time was increasingly limited, I had many sessions with each of the authors throughout the term, going over their manuscripts with them time and again, chapter by chapter, page by page, cutting here, adding there, substituting popular for psychological terms, shifting sentences and paragraphs, revising and further revising as needed. Our earlier emphasis had been on the traditional aspects of growing up in their tribes. Now the prospects of publication seemed to call for more pointed consideration of some of the changes taking place in the years since their own childhood.

To check first-hand the authenticity of our data, and to deepen our insights especially into the changing ways and needs of children and youth today, we arranged for several long week-end visits to the students' town and village homes, far from Kampala. These visits, which proved to be highlights of the season for all of us, provided an undergirding of reality and authenticity to what we were reading and writing, and certainly to our reasons for revising or adding to the papers.

I had deliberately encouraged these students to draw from their own experience. And this experience, in the case of each of them, must naturally include attitudes and feelings that the inherent continuity of such experience calls up. Indeed, if we are ever to get real insight into child development from this part of the world, complicated as it is by the psychological effects on the culture of decades of living under colonial rule, then surely an important value of this kind of writing, this reporting of a human life, is that it comes to us as seen through the eyes of the human being doing the living. Further, if we want such people to let us in on their thinking and feeling, whatever this may reveal of ambivalence, status-seeking, super-sensitivity, we will defeat our purpose by soft-pedalling or closing it off.

There should be no attempt to generalize from any one individual's experiences as seen in retrospect these several years later. That's why at least three versions of East African childhood have been included. There was to have been a fourth, about a Tanzanian childhood. But the student, for reasons unrelated to this project, withdrew his paper much too late in the process and the college term for another to be selected in its place.

It was a student from Tanzania (then Tanganyika), however, who, about half-way through the course, while chatting about his boyhood, made this statement: 'Strange as it may seem, I know more about my childhood now than I ever did. It's hard to believe, but through all these years of moving up through school, managing to do well in one State examination after another, I've felt that the little African boy I used to be has long since disappeared. In secondary school, and particularly now here at Makerere where we wear white shirts and speak English all the time, I've been saying to myself, "Yes, that little boy who herded the goats and skipped down the hill to carry messages for my father is no more; he's gone, completely gone." But now, you will be glad to hear, I know that isn't so. The little boy I used to be is part of me still, an important part. Many of the ways I now think and look at things that go on around me I can trace back in one way or another to my experiences as that African child.'

It is hoped that the readers, then, with deliberate thought and awareness, will accept this little book for what it is—the story of growing up in East Africa as seen through the eyes of three individuals, and recounted in the various ways they chose individually to write it—rather than to generalize from or argue about the validity of particular statements made by any one of them. It is hoped also that the book can help the readers in whatever writing they themselves may want to undertake, to compare and contrast these varied approaches and ways of writing, in terms of purpose, content, style, effect, as each looks back on his own years of growing up, to select the incidents of importance to him and hence worth the recording.

An East African student here in New York said the other day, on completing the reading of Nzioki's manuscript: 'Oh, I wish you would put back those missing early chapters. I didn't want the story to end. But since it *did* I just turned back to the beginning and read it a second time, chuckling just as hard as I had the first time. It reminds me so much of my own childhood, I can hardly believe it. Now I myself want to write.'

Other young Africans, and Asians as well, on reading one or more of the manuscripts, have made similar comment. It could be that the gentleman from the Kenya Institute of Education was right when he wrote: ' . . . I must say I enjoyed reading the stories. If they serve no other purpose I know they will inspire students to want to write about their own experiences, which might in time be the beginning of a wave of East African writing.'

We wish to acknowledge the help of, and extend our warmest thanks to:

The many people who have read the manuscripts and have given us the benefit of their insights and judgement;

Staff members of the Institute and of the Faculty of Education at Makerere University College, for encouraging our efforts all along and, more recently, during the editing process, for allowing us office space and the services of a typist;

The typist himself for working diligently and long to put the sometimes badly marked-up pages into readable typescript form;

Our classmate photographers listed overleaf and the Faculty of Education with whose permission the photographs are used in the book;

The administration of Queens College, City University of New York, for extending by six months my original year's leave of absence (as part of the A.I.D. Columbia University Teachers for East Africa Project) in order to continue work with the Bachelor of Education programme;

The editors of Oxford University Press in Nairobi, for their advice and help;

Indeed, all friends who, in whatever way, have helped to make this venture an exciting one throughout!

Professor of Education　　　　　　LORENE K. FOX, Ph.D.
Queens College of the　　　　　　*New York City*
City University of New York;　　　*June, 1966.*
Visiting Professor, 1962-64
National Institute of Education, 1966-67,
Makerere University College.

NOTE: We are grateful also to those authors whose works have been of such valuable help and inspiration to this project, especially those who have written about African children and youth, including Dr. F. J. Bennett,* Dr. Meyer Fortes, Dr. D. B. Jelliffe,* Dr. Barrington Kaye, H. E. Mzee Jomo Kenyatta, Mr. Camara Laye, Drs. Barbara and Robert Levine, Mr. Albert Maleche,* Dr. S. H. Ominde and Dr. Otto Raum.

Most of the photographs used in the book were taken by students other than the authors. Hence they are *not* autobiographical, but were selected because they are characteristic also of the life described in the text. Exceptions are: photographs L3 and L11, which *were* taken of the Abaluyia, A20 and Mr. Ocitti's which *were* taken in Acholi.

Those who took the photographs are: D. K. Aneco, L. K. Fox, J. M. Githaiga, J. A. Lijembe, Fr. J. M. Lwanga, J. K. Mugenzi, Fr. P. Ngondwe, J. P. Ocitti and M. Ssengooba-Ssebanakitta.

All of the photographs, appearing between pages 66 and 67, and through publishers' oversight not numbered, are listed below in their order, and identified with the photographers' names:

Lijembe 1.	'. . . I would hold her arms . . .	(Ocitti)
L 2.	Then, as now, before the baby . . .	(Githaiga)
L 3.	The girls' would have with them . . .	(Lijembe)
L 4.	The duty of collecting and carrying . . .	(Mugenzi)
L 5.	'We would make use of . . .	(Ocitti)
L 6.	'Whoever hit the target . . .	(Ocitti)
L 7.	Boys with no older sister . . .	(Ocitti)
L 8.	Today 'the child enters school . . .	(Ocitti)
L 9.	'Radios these days . . .	(Aneco)
L10.	'Travel for many youngsters . . .	(Lwanga)
L11.	'Fathers now take a keener interest . . .	(Fox)
L12.	Increasingly, both new and expectant . . .	(Mugenzi)
Apoko 13.	'. . . Lapidi (the nurse) is the second . . .	(Ocitti)
A14.	'A mother who does not have lapidi . . .	(Ocitti)
A15.	'At meal time all children . . .	(Ocitti)
A16.	They 'like to pull grasses . . .	(Aneco)
A17.	Girls who attend secondary . . .	(Ngondwe)
A18.	The thirteen-to-sixteen-year-old . . .	(Ocitti)
A19.	'By this time (from the age of . . .	(Ocitti)
A20.	'Often it seems to be only . . .	(Fox)
Nzioki 21.	Then, as now, every new-born . . .	(Ocitti)
N22.	Small boys would play . . .	(Githaiga)
N23.	How often a first-born son . . .	(Ssengooba-Ssebanakitta)
N24.	Herding was after all a pleasant . . .	(Mugenzi)

Futher errata: On page 115, line 12 and page 116, line 20, and on page 129, line 8, 'White' should read 'white'. On page 104, line 1, 'tight' should read 'tightly'.

* also served our class as guest lecturer on one or more occasions (as did Mrs. Alisi Mujunga and Mr. Barnabas Otaala, to whom we are indebted).

THE VALLEY BETWEEN:

A Muluyia's Story

by
Joseph A. Lijembe

1.

Birth and Infancy

My mother had had two daughters before my arrival. My father's kinsfolk all hoped that the next birth would bring a boy, and my father confirms that if I had turned out to be a baby girl, he would have seriously considered looking for another wife who, as he thought, would have given him male offspring. Both of my sisters died long before I was aware there had been any children before me.

According to Luyia custom, husbands must not be seen around at the time of delivery, though they are to be informed immediately by messenger of the sex of the infant. My father tells me, however, that being anxious to know the sex of his new-born baby, he lingered around the home during this birth, pretending to be doing some useful work, so that as soon as the attendants left the place he would find out at once. When he learned that his new baby was a boy, he admits, he could not help pushing the customary practice aside. Usually, fathers do not touch *tsingukuni*, the new-born, until in some cases two months after the birth. Three reasons were given me for this practice: (1) normally the father would have to be away fighting much of the time, and therefore he could not commit himself to becoming fond of his children; (2) since the infant always remained naked, it was felt that the father should give himself time during which the child's skin would turn 'black'; and (3) his touching the young baby would be taken as a sign that the husband wished to 'see' his wife again.

Thus, ignoring all the taboos of the tribe, my father was my first visitor, holding me in his arms with happiness, all the time thinking what lucky names he would give to his new-born son. The names he chose, it was believed, must be agreeable to the ancestral spirits; for if the spirits did not approve of the names given they would make the young baby cry to death. My father chose three names for me: Muloli, my grandfather's name, Shigogodi, a local hero's name, and Lijembe, which in English means 'hoe'! (The idea here was that my father had just purchased such an implement from an Asian shop-owner at Kakamega for the purpose of cultivating his *shamba*. In fact, he may have been one of the first farmers in the area to use this new implement.) I am told I would stop crying only when my third name, Lijembe, was called, so that the other two names became less frequently used. The habit of naming a child after his father is a borrowed one, and has come into use in our tribe very recently.

I am told that I was breast-fed by my mother until I was able to sit up alone, when millet porridge and eventually solid food also were introduced into my diet. The tribe believes that growing children, beginning as early as possible, should be fed in this way in order to toughen the growing bones. Also, it was the duty of the mother to see that the child suckled as much milk as possible. The Abidakho believe that the more milk a child suckles from the mother the more breath the child will have later on for blowing up fire in the fire-place. My mother must have made sure that I had enough; because one of the duties she was delighted to see me perform a few years later was that of making a fire and keeping it burning throughout the cooking period.

I am told I was a very sleepy baby and gave very little trouble to my mother. Once she fed me, I would simply sleep, and sleep for many hours, while she went about her domestic duties. Most babies in Idakho would wear no clothes; they would be sheltered close to the mother during cold weather and through the nights. Usually a mother would wear a simple sheet for her dress, and the same sheet would be used as a blanket at night. This blanket would be shared by the baby; for it was the duty of the mother to sleep with the young children at night, providing bodily warmth and attending to them when they were wet or hungry. The father would sleep on his 'bed' alone, and would invite neither the child nor the mother to this bed until after he had touched the new-born baby.

My parents made a point of introducing me to their various kinsmen. Visits to relatives would be made 'officially' on three occasions: (1) when the child was about a month old, (2) when the child was teething, and (3) when the child was able to talk. Gifts for each occasion were different, by custom. I am told that my first visit was to my maternal home, where I was showered with various gifts, one of which had to be a cow. (This cow was to remain in our home until I was old enough to see it and decide what to do with it). The visits to my father's relatives were arranged as soon as I had been introduced to my mother's relatives. An important point about our society is that a wife becomes more closely linked with her husband's kinship with each child she bears. Similarly the man acquires seniority in the society through every child raised. These visits served as a means of informing especially the distant relatives that their lineage was steadily being extended.

An Idakho mother usually weans her child as soon as she feels he is 'mature enough' or big enough to eat the same food the family eats and no longer to require a mother's constant care, or when she realizes that she is pregnant again. At this time she will use either tobacco juice or hot pepper on her breasts to scare off the child. Alternatively she will send the child away to some relatives' home for a brief stay. I was still suckling my mother's breasts, I am told, at the age of three years. Then one day as I started to suckle I suddenly tasted an unusual bitterness. Startled, and whimpering, I was afraid of touching my mother's breasts ever again. Shortly after this, I was sent abruptly to my maternal uncle's home for a period of many months. When I came back, I found that my little sister, Mang'ong'o Alusa, had arrived.

2.

The Little Boy 'Nurse'

I was not yet four years old when my sister was born. I had got used to sleeping away from my mother's care, having been so long with my uncle. On my return, together with other male youngsters of very nearly the same age, I began to sleep in my grandfather's hut. (The girls of this age also would sleep away from their parents' homes and at some grandmother's house.) Because there was no older sister in the family, and my mother had to go off to work in the *shamba* every day, it wasn't long before I was obliged, though still a very young child myself, to become the day-to-day 'nurse' for my baby sister. For my mother to make me succeed in this function, she had to train me— to give me instructions and to see how well I carried them out. I had at first to do some of the things while she watched—feed the child on porridge, for example. Such training took us into the planting season of the following year. As her *shamba* work increased, so did my nursing duties.

In our home the day would start with early morning duties for all the members of our household except the baby, Mang'ong'o Alusa. My father would put out our animals, which included cows, goats and sheep. He would then sharpen the farm tools and go to the farm, very often without breakfast. My mother would fetch water from the river, clean *shiko*, that area of the house occupied by our domestic animals at night, and breast-feed Alusa. On my arrival from Grandfather's hut, which used to be at sunrise, I would be sent to look for fire from other homes; if, that is, my mother had been careless about keeping hers burning through the night. I would build or stir up the fire in the fire-place, and leave it for my mother to make breakfast. This breakfast was of maize meal, which was meant for my father. I would be asked to eat *bujeni*, the remains of the previous day's supper. My mother would check Alusa's porridge, which had been made out of millet flour and stored in a gourd for ready use. Sometimes the porridge turned out to be sour, but it would still serve the purpose, my mother believed. She would then wake up the baby to give her the last feed for the morning. And lastly, before moving off to the *shamba*, she would give me instructions: Do not leave the home unguarded, she would tell me, for fear that thieves would steal our property. Do not leave Alusa crying for long periods of time, for that would be dangerous to her health. Feed her when she cries. Guard the chickens from wild cats and the chicks from wild birds. Be helpful to visitors and strangers who ask you for information. Finally, she would promise to bring me a present—a piece of fruit, a potato—when she returned from work. Then she would leave, not to return until very late in the evening.

As soon as my mother left, loneliness would set in. I was in charge of a huge house and, judged by present day standards, it was a very dark, extremely untidy and even filthy house. The outside was frightful, too. There were known to be wild cats which would come to catch our chickens. Thieves might come at any moment, too. All of these thoughts would frighten me constantly in my early days of home-guarding and baby-nursing.

As Alusa slept for long hours, I would decide to do some of the things I had seen my mother do, but which she had not particularly asked me to do. I had seen her grind millet and prepare and cook bananas; so I would keep busy with one or two of these jobs until Alusa would wake up. Then I would feed her according to instructions: shake the gourd that contained the porridge, lay Alusa on my lap with the head resting on my stomach, fold my left palm and fingers so as to make a curved cup to be placed below her mouth. Into this curve I would pour porridge until her mouth was submerged. As soon as the porridge touched her mouth, Alusa would suck it in. If she refused to suck it, I had been told to stop feeding her. But, of course, I had noticed my mother force the baby to suck by closing her nostrils with a finger, thereby forcing her to breathe through the mouth. As the mouth was submerged in porridge, the breathing would inevitably force the porridge down the gullet. At first I feared trying this trick; I would simply hold her until my mother returned from work.

Sooner or later, I discovered that in the meantime I could go away and—when Alusa was sleeping—play with other 'nurses' from the neighbouring homes. At first we were afraid to go because our parents had given us strict orders to remain at home. But having established among us the place where we would play whenever a chance came, we would gather there as soon as possible after the parents had gone to the *shambas*.

Here we would come with our siblings. We would sit them

or lay them on the ground and the five of us would go on playing. We would attend to our babies only when they cried excessively. Then we would sing lullabies to make them go to sleep quickly, hurriedly feed them, or perhaps tie them, still crying, on our backs and continue playing. Neither our babies nor we ourselves had any clothes to put on, so there was no problem of washing napkins! Neither were children and babies supposed to be bathed lest they catch disease. Yet when we did try to bathe ourselves as well as the babies, the only objection our parents would raise was that the process involved our leaving the homes unguarded. This was true, since we had to do the bathing at a river, where we energetically engaged ourselves in play activity. As the four of my playmates were girls, they would have with them containers in which to draw water, thereby helping the mothers in other home duties as well as nursing.

Another activity of ours was that of collecting and carrying firewood. At first I was reluctant to take part in this because it was felt essentially to be girls' work. But my mother encouraged me to do it—in fact at one stage she threatened to refuse me food if I did not bring firewood during the day! Games such as hide-and-seek, and 'make-believe' play—imitating mother at cooking, death ceremonies, riddles, house-building (using maize-cobs), harvesting, beer-party scenes, circumcision ceremonies—all of these would engage our energies and vigour as we guarded the homes and cared for the babies.

It was my duty as Alusa's nurse to offer her toilet 'training'. For toilet paper, I was instructed to use *mavuya*, a special type of leaf, soft enough to resemble the feel of our present-day toilet paper. Nurses were all instructed to use *mavuya* whenever babies defecated. As Alusa grew older she was usually told, either by my mother or by myself, to excrete on the grass. But many children in our location, fearing the cool dew in the early morning, would go alongside the house, or even in the house itself. There were no latrines as such; grown-ups went into the bush. Hence there was always an uncultivated piece of land near the home for this purpose.

When my mother returned from work, she would look round the house and at the baby to see if I had done my duty well. If Alusa's eyes were red, she would know Alusa had cried a lot during the day. If the gourd was still full of porridge, she would know Alusa had not been fed. She would then deduce that I had left her uncared for and had gone off to play. I would be reported to my father who would decide the punishment for the offence and who would inflict that punishment, usually a beating. If all was well, on the other hand, my mother would breast-feed Alusa, lay her down to rest, and begin to prepare our evening meal. I would be released to go out and play with the other children.

Through the years, I continued as a nurse—with more experience, of course, since I also was growing older. The number of my playmates also increased. As Alusa grew bigger, I had to help her in sitting up, providing the support until she was able to sit by herself. During her crawling period, the period when children desire to reach out, and to test everything with the mouth, I had to be on constant watch. As she began toddling, I had to 'train' her until she could walk on her own. This latter training had two or three stages. First, while supporting her feet on the ground, I would hold her arms and with a tune, 'Teee teee teee,' make her feet move one after the other. Second-ly, a little later, I would provide a stick on to which she would hold, and as I moved it slowly, she would follow. During this stage, too, I would let her support herself along the wall of the house and I would provide encouragement for her to move towards me or some other object. There was another nurse whose sibling took longer to walk, and I noticed that the nurse would put the little one on the dewy grass during the early morning hours and make the child move its feet in the cold dew for an hour or so. This was supposed to strengthen the feet of the toddler and thus speed up the walking process.

Before Alusa was a year old, her breast-feeding was supple-mented with solid foods, just as mine had been a few years before. The first of these foods was banana. My mother would chew the banana until it was ready for swallowing, remove it from her own mouth, and give it to Alusa in small bits. This practice would be highly unwelcome today; but it was the way the parents in Idakho society imagined babies without teeth and without strong chewing muscles should be fed on solids. Later black *bushuma*, made out of millet flour, was introduced and this when given to the baby would not have been chewed by a grown up. Instead, it would be given along with some slippery type of vegetable called *lihu* which made swallowing without chewing easy.

As I had to use these solids as well as the porridge for feeding Alusa, I found that my responsibilities as a nurse increased.

During the day I would prepare and cook bananas in order to provide a meal not only for Alusa but for myself and my playmates as well. This was a risky business. Many a time in those days nurses had been known to set houses on fire while cooking in the absence of grown ups. If I was going to cook bananas, say, for Alusa and me, I would have to find firewood, to fetch water from the river, to wash the cutlery after using it, to feed Alusa, to use a knife without harming myself, to place dangerous materials out of Alusa's reach, and to allow myself time for play. How well I remember one particular time when I had prepared porridge for our lunch. As I was dishing it out on the plates, the container slipped and both my hands were covered with hot porridge! By the time a neighbour arrived to cool my hands with wet soil, I had had enough pain to teach me always to fear touching anything hot.

3.

Children's Groups at Home and at Play

I have already referred to the make-believe play in which I took part with my playmates while nursing. We would make use of such simple materials as sand, soil, bricks, stones, string, sticks, bottles, banana balls, banana ends, hoops, maize-cobs, baskets, certain grasses, green branches, catapults, bows and arrows, and drums.

Evening was a favourite time for the children of the village to come together in an open area to play. At this time boys and girls who had accompanied their parents to the *shambas* during the day, the boys who had been with the herds, and the nurses (mostly girls) would meet to play. At first the whole group would take part in a collective game, such as *shilemba;* or the depicting of a circumcision ceremony; or *wetee*, a signal for the start of a mock beer-party session. Later, nurses and older children would break into separate groups of their own; and as it got darker, girls and boys would play separately. As soon as one member of the play-group was called home, everything would come to an end.

From our work we would usually go home in groups of three or four; in fact we were not expected to arrive home without friends. This was particularly true if we had gone to *mmasitsa*, a weekly social gathering taking place on Sunday afternoons at a fixed place, *Ikambi*. At *Ikambi* youngsters would generally take part in such activities as dancing to *isukudi*, a drum-like instrument, or they would simply mix with the crowds gathered there, as they were expected to make friends with other children and youths from all over the location. Returning from such occasions then, we would visit the three or four homes in turn, sharing the food which had been prepared and kept for the nurse-member of the family.

Later on, as my sister Alusa was growing up, my mother had to keep two separate dishes for us. Alusa would have her own group of girls who would eat by themselves, normally near the cooking place and supervised by the mother. My group and I would eat in what would be the sitting room, on our own; if my father was around he would take care of us. As for 'eating manners,' these had to be instilled in us by our grandfather at whose house we slept at night. We would then move from our home to another one, until the homes of the members of the group had all been visited. In this way we came to know, and appreciate or dislike, the particular treatment meted out in the different homes in our neighbourhood.

Perhaps I ought to mention that the whole group of us would eat from one common plate for the main meal, usually maize-meal, and from another common dish for vegetables. If meat was available, mothers would make a special point of giving each individual his or her own piece of meat beforehand. In the case of one member of the group taking a lion's share of the vegetables, the grandfather or grandmother was instructed by the parents to stress the idea of 'honesty' when next he or she met the children. I remember that in 1943, when I was a boy of eleven, there was widespread famine in Kenya. One day my step-mother gave my group some food which we had to eat in the dark. My friends washed their hands first and fell to the dish; before I could settle down to join them the dishes were literally empty. In anger I refused to join the group for a tour of the remaining homes. Instead I stayed at home, to wait for the time my father would have his supper. Fathers in our community ate their meals last and would always share their portion of food with any of the children who seemed hungry after their first round.

At a later stage in our growing up, there were three periods in the day when we children would normally be released by our parents for play, or when we would be expected to be playing. The first came during the morning and midday hours, when we would play at a grazing ground. With a huge wide field before us, we herdsboys would still make use of the toys listed earlier, especially bows and arrows and catapults. This was my favourite 'game'. We would aim at a particular target—a bush, a tree, a rock, a bird—and attempt to hit it. Whoever hit the target at first attempt would be exempt from some of the numerous duties that had to do with herding. This was the time when, and the place where, we also organized 'bull-fighting,' using 'bulls' made out of clay, *viyumbu* (banana ends) or *luseso* (a certain tough grass). In the fields, too, we would play *idiolo* and *ikhuya*, which resemble the Western game of hockey except that maize-cobs were used instead of balls. This was the time when, out of green branches, we would build *madili*, or temporary houses, and pretend we were shelter-ing, sleeping, or even cooking in them. We would also practise 'warring' tactics, which sometimes included being forced by the group to remain in the rain as long as it lasted, to swim across the fairly fast-flowing River Yala in order to escape from an attack by other youngsters, to climb a thorn tree, or to run through a prickly bush. Sometimes out of the mouth of the biggest youngster in the group would come the music of *isukudi*, when we would all be required to dance. While the boys were out on the grazing field, the girls would usually be helping their mothers in the gardens or at home, or occupying themselves with 'housekeeping' play somewhere nearby on the compound.

Even today, Idakho youngsters still find time to go into the open field and practise most of these games. They still go out to hunt birds and small animals, to fish along the streams, to slide down a slope while seated on slippery portions of banana tree. In my day we would do most of these things near a spring or a stream so we could have a bath afterwards. Nowadays, many of the younger participants, at least, go home for their nurses or mothers to bathe them.

The second of the play periods would come later in the day. After we had come back from herding, and the girls had returned from the gardens, we would gather at an open area again, this time not very far from our homes. The main game at this time, usually around four o'clock, might be a kind of tennis for boys and perhaps throwing-and-catching for girls, both groups making use of banana balls. This would go on till supper time.

After supper, we would gather for our third play adventure of the day, this time at our *tsisimba*. For a brief period boys and girls would mix to play *kongolo*, a game related to some childless beast which was meant to kill its friends' children. We would also take part together in hide-and-seek games. As it got darker, however, we would be asked by our guardians to separate. At our separate *tsisimba*, we would sometimes engage in story-telling; sometimes in *ing'ombe*, discovering by guess work in which hand an object had been hidden; or in *shitandawili-ndega*, which included riddles. This was frequently a time also for listening to direct instructions from our guardians. The boys would remain out of doors a little longer to do traditional dances involving *shilemba*, a traditional burial of an important old man, or *bukhulu*, that which pertains to circumcision rituals.

Looking back, I know now that through these play activities I developed my imagination, made discoveries about the world of nature, and gained important social skills, usually finding myself organizing and generally taking the leadership of my group of playmates.

4.

Learning Through Work

Throughout early childhood, as already described, with no older sister in the family, it fell to my lot to take on the duties of a nurse for my young sister and to help with other duties around the home—gathering fire-wood, stirring the cooking fire, fetching water, sweeping the compound, preparing food for my sister and me, guarding the home, and other such work usually learned and performed by the girls of the tribe in preparation for womanhood. After the age of about eight, I was required to assume specific responsibilities deemed appropriate for boys. My father would send me to represent him at a communal house-building project. This used to be, and still is, a very common function in our society. The older folk at the project would accept a child's presence only if they were certain of his physical constitution. Once accepted, it was a test for me to work hard so that I could continue to be at such meetings. My father would also send me on important journeys and errands. Before he could send me, though, he would need to be sure that I could run very fast on being attacked by other youngsters on the way, that I was honest and obedient and, if the errand was for reporting death in the family, that I knew how to give the message, expressing it first through cries, then mentioning names. Once, I remember, my father sent me to invite a male relative for a discussion on dowry. On finding the man absent, I gave the message to his wife. This was 'wrong'; invitations of this kind must reach the man from another man or male youngster, and not from any female. As a result of my mistake, the relative never turned up, and the crucial discussion had to be postponed indefinitely. My father was very angry, and I thought he would punish me severely. He spared me.

Another important activity in which I participated centred on garden work. I used to accompany my father to the *shamba* very early in the morning. There I would help him in clearing the bush so that my mother would find it easy to dig. Boys would only clear the grass; they would not help in digging as this was essentially girls' work. Later I joined a group of youngsters who had formed *buhasyo*, for co-operative efforts. One morning we would work for one member and the next for another, and so on. After clearing, and still working in *buhasyo*, we would take up weeding and later go on to harvesting and storing, especially of maize.

Girls would also organize *buhasyo* and do most of the digging and planting. While girls would carry the maize seeds in baskets on their heads from the garden to the store, boys would normally do so on their backs, using sacks.

Herding was another essential activity in the location. It was the favourite work of most boys, of course, allowing us much time and freedom for group play as described.

5.

Moral Training

Since moral training was part and parcel of every aspect of traditional education passed on by generation after generation of Baluyia parents to their children, it seems hardly necessary to deal with it as something apart. Tribal education, as these pages have shown, was learning through experience in the main at almost every stage, with the parents, especially the mother, coming to the aid of the learner only when a mistake had been made somewhere. My childhood years as a nurse are illustrative of this kind of learning. So is the work we did in the garden and out with the herds in the field. Although this practical training was deemed highly important for children, and certainly the parents made it perfectly clear, through their systems of threats and punishment, just which were the wrong and which the right ways of doing such tasks, still they seemed to have something else in mind for 'moral training.' Morals and manners were felt by the Baluyia, it seems, to be closely related if not synonymous. Great stress was put on outside behaviour. What one was *seen* doing was what seemed to count in the development of character—instilled by maxim, by proverbs, by stories and riddles, or by direct oral instruction; all of this reinforced, as always, through the regular use of fear and punishment.

Children were trained from their earliest years to be respectful, obedient, and mannerly, these being the standards by which adults became acceptable to society. All parents, and fathers in particular, were very stern with children who in any way departed from such standards. Furthermore, the punishment for children who misbehaved, however harsh, had to be accepted by them without question or complaint. Thus the children, respectfully submissive, learned to fear their fathers as harsh and severe, being called upon in their positions as heads of the family to punish whatever serious misbehaviour they themselves observed or was reported by the mothers. Strong feelings of dislike, though dutifully suppressed, were very frequently mixed in with this fear. I remember one occasion when my playmate decided to 'punish' his father by removing his working tools from the place where they were usually kept, thereby upsetting the time-table for the father's *shamba* work. The youngster had no other way of expressing his resentment of the father's strictness and harshness.

Children's relations with the mother—although she too could be quick to punish, sometimes severely—were much closer in general than with the father, particularly in the earlier years. There was more love for and dependence on the mother. The father's authority over the mother too was absolute, even legal. Baluyia men were entitled and frequently known to punish their wives whenever the wives displeased them in some way. I remember once as a young child returning from *isimba* to find my mother crying outside the house. Out of sheer emotion I also started crying, thereby showing my sympathy for my mother. When my father emerged from the house, he tried to separate me from my mother who was then holding me firmly. He failed to separate us. As a result he slapped both of us in fury and ordered us to be away from his sight. Later that day we made off for my mother's home where we stayed for a period. The point here was that, as a boy, I was to sympathize with my father, regardless of whether or not my mother was wrong. As I did not do this, I received the same punishment as my mother. We were both banished to her home to learn better manners. Also in those days, whenever a husband inflicted a punishment on his wife, he did it publicly, partly to impress on her the seriousness of her wrong-doing, and partly to add to his own stature and reputation in the eyes of others, particularly of the women about the home. Older brothers, by virtue of their seniority as well as of their male superiority, were quite free to punish or demand obedience from younger brothers or sisters whenever they chose, and sometimes even from their mothers.

We were taught to respect our elders at all times and be very particular about our manners in their presence. I came to know at an early age that it was proper for us children to extend our greetings to visitors who came to the home only after the visitors had been seated and our parents had greeted them. Shortly after such greetings, it did not take me long to learn, we were to withdraw from the adult company at once and under no circumstances were we to join in or even listen to their conversations. By about the age of seven I had learned too that it was wrong to greet strangers or persons who had not entered the house. Whenever my mother would hear me shouting greetings to passers-by, she would rebuke me, explaining that strangers were known to kidnap friendly children, thus instilling fear into me.

Yes, fear played a big part in the growing up of all of us from a very young age. Whenever my baby sister Alusa refused to suckle, I remember, my mother always forced her to do so by slapping her. If she continued to cry for a long time she would be 'thrown' out in the dark and my mother would invite *manani*, some wild beasts, to 'come and eat her!' I am told this used to happen to me also. Then later, whenever I refused to do any duty allocated by my mother, she would threaten to report me to my father, who would give me a thorough beating on hearing of my unco-operativeness. As I grew older and had to sleep outside our home, I found it frightening to move about at night. I had to be given escort by either my mother or my father. I was afraid of the existence of night-runners, wild beasts, and even ghosts which my parents used to say haunted our home area.

I remember one time, too, that my father came home with his leg bandaged. He had been bitten by a snake while gathering posts for putting up a cow *boma*. Fortunately he killed the snake, but unfortunately he brought it along. It is believed in my society that if children urinate in their beds at night, they can be cured of the habit if a dead snake is tied round their waists. I feared not only that the snake would be tied round my waist. I was terrified by even the sight of it, and ran out of the house with the loudest cry I can ever recall making.

About the same year, I remember, I once helped myself to *shihango*, the roasted meat that is kept for emergency cases, without the permission of my mother. When she came home and discovered that the hidden treasure had been removed and eaten, she did not wait to report me to my father. She gave me a thorough beating then and there, threatening to cut off my hands, these being the limbs I had used for stealing! In that moment I learned not to steal, although just how lasting the learning was I cannot say.

The way the moral training was carried out by various Idakho homes would necessarily be different and often inconsistent. For example, in my case, there were moments when my father or mother, separately or jointly, would rebuke or punish me for something they had never told me was wrong. There were other times when I would receive the closest attention when, by crying, I showed them that I had done a 'wrong' thing. Moreover, everywhere in our community, it was difficult for children to know which was the accepted way of expressing respect towards their parents until, as in my case, I had acted one way or another, and had been rebuked or, less frequently, praised. In homes where there was constant quarrelling between father and mother, or between a parent and older children, young boys and girls would often become confused and fearful, which made the process of training them to respect their parents in particular, and grown ups generally, a difficult task. In other words, parents very largely disciplined their children without knowing that they themselves may have had a part to play in many of the mistakes for which the children were being punished.

Occasions when the family gathered round the courtyard fire, after the evening meal, afforded a very common opportunity for moral training among the Baluyia and, for all of us children, a favourite one. Stories of animals or people, stressing the 'rightness' of certain traits which always won out, and the 'wrongness' of others which more than met their just deserts, kept even the youngest of us trying to blink away the late hour's sleepiness. We wanted to hear the oft familiar ending of the story and the very subtle, not always understandable, proverb or moral with which the elder story-teller would give the final dramatic touch.

As we approached adolescence, we would be sent by our parents to selected elders, men and women of outstanding position in the location, whose function was to start training us, by social maxim and direct instruction, for future parenthood and adult behaviour in the tribe. The natural and social conditions peculiar to the location and development of the tribe itself often dictated the particular values to be stressed. It was a matter of necessity, for example, that Luyia boys should be taught to be courageous, because the Abaluyia were constantly being attacked by the Kalenjin from the east and the Luo from the west. Our earlier warlike play, already described, had often included attacks against or from the Kalenjin or Luo, as well as the traditional victory songs sung lustily by the small 'warriors'. It was also important for the children and youth to value heroism, because it was only after a series of acts of heroism that a Muluyia could acquire status sufficient for having his or her name taken on by new-born babies after the hero's death. All of these matters the selected tutors, in their seasoned manner, would bring home to us as we made our way to manhood and womanhood, rounding out the long years of traditional education so effectively instilled in us.

6.

Location and Tribe

The Abidakho are a section of the Luyia tribe. The Abaluyia occupy the three counties of Bungoma, Busia and Kakamega, which form the Western Province of Kenya. This province, traversed by the Rivers Yala, Isiukhu, and Nzoia, forms a basin—the valley between—bounded by Mt. Elgon to the north, by the Nandi Escarpment to the east, and stretching westwards to Lake Victoria. The Abaluyia are divided into locations of varying size and population. The Abidakho live in Idakho Location, one of the smallest locations in the county of Kakamega. It lies to the south of Kakamega, the administrative centre of the province. The location covers an area of about 200 square miles, and has a population of about 40,000 citizens.

The Abidakho, together with five other sections of the Luyia tribe, have the characteristic use of 'kh' in their dialect. This linguistic difference does not isolate these sections from the rest of the tribe. It merely distinguishes them from the others without hampering communication.

The Abidakho are both pastoral and agricultural. They keep cattle, sheep and goats. These animals are, of course, not only a source of wealth, but also a store of wealth. The more cattle a man has the more wealthy he is and, therefore, the more influential he is in the society. As well as being the source and store of wealth, these animals are used for bride-price purposes. Also they provide meat, milk and skins. These days oxen are used for ploughing purposes. Poultry used to be kept as a ready means for use as meat whenever a home received visitors at unexpected times, and as gifts for friends and relatives of a home to take away with them after paying a visit. These days, too, but beginning with those earlier times, we have learnt to put eggs to commercial uses in addition to eating them ourselves.

On the farms or *shambas* we grow maize, our chief crop, and millet, beans, sweet potatoes and cassava. Each homestead has a banana plantation behind it. Well-to-do families have started growing such cash crops as coffee, tea and sugar cane.

Like all other Abaluyia of my generation, we had our two lower central incisors removed. The process is still applied to a small number of youngsters in Idakho at the age of five or six, but by a 'specialist'. The purpose of this practice originally, I am told, was to provide an opening in the mouth for *luseshe*—a siphon, made for use especially by the beer-party participants. Further, by custom, when an important person died, he would be buried in a sitting position, with such a siphon stuck in his mouth at one end, and the other end placed in a pot containing beer. The opening between the teeth, of course, would hold the tube in position. It is not surprising that, with the coming of European missionaries this custom has been gradually dying out. The well-known practices pertaining to circumcision and initiation rites are still common to much of the tribe although, again, the manner and importance of these ceremonies are changing with time.

In the field of sports, the Abidakho were traditionally great warriors, great hunters and great dancers. Our traditional dance was done to the *isukudi*, to whose beat the 'natives' would dance in a very fashionable and vigorous manner. The location has twice put on shows of *isukudi* for British royal visitors, and on many occasions *isukudi* dancers have been called to Jamhuri Park (formerly Mitchell Park), Nairobi, to give performances during the days when the Kenya Royal Agricultural Show was in progress. We also still enjoy on occasion a turn of bull-fighting—a sport that seems to have reached us from the coast where the Portuguese first introduced it in the seventeenth century. At the beginning of each year we have *mukoye*, a wrestling festival, when the youth of the location participate in the tactics of wrestling. For many years also the Kenya football team, competing for the East African trophy, Gossage, has depended on the skilful leadership of a Mwidakho.

Missionary activities—the most important one being managing primary and intermediate schools in the location—are carried out by three main groups: the Catholics, the Quakers, and the Anglicans.

7.

Traditional Attitudes Towards Marriage and Family

From the interviews I had with the Chief's Council of Elders, with various village elders—and other individuals—including my father, aged about sixty, it is clear, looking back into time, that a Mwidakho who wished to obtain the maximum degree of protection by the community and to attain a position of influence and prestige in it, has always done so mainly through marriage and procreation. I was told again and again that the older a person grows, and the wider becomes the group of people related to him by blood and by marriage, the wider, accordingly, extends his 'sphere of influence'. Seniority in Idakho does not consist in mere accumulation of years, but in the increasing number of effective kinship relations involved in the process of ageing. Thus, the recognition my father holds in the society is directly dependent on the number of children he has been able to raise from his marriage. This recognition is further enhanced by the fact that he is able to see his grandchildren from time to time.

Marriage, it was stressed repeatedly, is the way through which young people gain independence from their parents. Generally, the unmarried youth has been dependent on his or her parents in every respect: tilling his father's land and eating his mother's food, thereby being completely under his parents' authority, and having no independent status with regard to property. Marriage for such a youth has meant the gradual gaining of personal independence.

As the newly married couple frequently has not, and could not, set up a new home of their own immediately, marriage has been a welcome idea to the family because, through it, the boy's parents have received an additional household servant. For the first year or two, sometimes longer, the son's new wife was expected to submit to her mother-in-law's authority. She had to perform all the pleasant and unpleasant duties of her in-law's home. Her being accepted as a daughter-in-law in the young man's home depended importantly on her conduct during this period and on how well she performed the duties assigned her. As if in exchange for these economic and domestic services, the girl's home received bride price in the form of three milking cows, one bull, two goats, two sheep, and a set of beads. Money as we know it today was not involved when such a bride price was first settled upon.

I was reminded, too, that in earlier days the relationship between man and wife became fully established only after the birth of a child or of several children. Only then did the society consider the bond between husband and wife as permanent. Generally both parents looked forward to having many children, because the society believed that a large family enhanced a man's prestige; through it, his name became known to many people who, accordingly, respected him and listened to him. They also considered that a man with many children could obtain justice. He would be feared, so that people would not dare to take his cattle or other property away by force. It was also desirable to have many children because, with their co-operation in the home, there would always be plenty of food.

Opinions differed among my fellow tribesmen regarding which sex the society preferred. Some said that a home with more sons than daughters was more respected than a home with a few or no sons at all. The Chief's Council was of the opinion that the stress was on as many children as possible in each home, and that it was considered bad luck if a family raised only girls.

The idea being to raise as many children as possible, it was considered a serious disadvantage for a man to have a wife who was barren. It was serious too when it was the husband who was discovered to be impotent, although he could secretly request a brother or other male relative or friend to father his children for him.

It is at birth, as the account of my advent into the family and tribe has made clear, that Baluyia children are socially accepted and accorded a place in the community. Indeed, child-birth is a highly welcome event in our society, where only through parenthood can men and women achieve honoured status. Not even the introduction of European schools has done much as yet to detract from this ideal.

8.

At Primary School

When I was almost ten years old, the Chief issued a decree in the location that all children who were capable of herding cattle should now go to school. And so one morning the Chief's *askaris* collected my group of youngsters (pulling them out of bed when necessary), and later that morning—a misty and rainy morning in November, I remember—about thirty of us were recruited for our village school. All of us were rough and unkempt, and without clothes. We came from homes where the teachings of Christianity had not penetrated. What a picture we must have given of frightfulness and disturbance, to the teachers and to the orderliness of the 'school'! It was not a school, actually, for the first two years, but only an open compound where classes were held. We sat on the ground, I remember, learning to write in the soil with our fingers or with small sticks. Beginning with the third year, those of us who wished to continue had to move on to a larger school with some classrooms, many miles from our village.

The adjustments we were called on to make were not easy. At home I had had to be seen and not heard; children never talked freely in the presence of adults. When I went to school it took me a long time to adjust myself to the new environment. At first I was shy about talking to my teachers, who always encouraged me to look at them as I spoke or answered their questions in the class.

At home I had learned that fathers were punishing and not loving persons. Experience had taught me to obey male adults for fear of being punished. My respect and loyalty to them had been a matter of force. How would this affect my relationship with the teachers? I had to learn at school that it was not necessary to fear the male teachers, provided that I carried out my duties satisfactorily. It was perhaps the fact that I had been sadly deprived of much early close contact with my mother—by her being away in the garden throughout the day, by my sleeping away from the home at night, and by the arrival of another child while I was still very young—that contributed to my tendency to lean toward the women teachers in the school. My continued and pleasant association, as a child nurse, with the group of little girl nurses during much of this time, may also have made a difference here.

The school, being missionary-sponsored, insisted on honesty as the key to citizenship. The home also insisted on honesty. But I had seen in my home, and in many other homes as well, dishonest practices, such as telling lies, thieving, and so on, sometimes praised and at other times despised. For example, stealing cattle from the Kalenjin homes across the Nandi Escarpment was accepted as a 'heroic' act; and telling lies in order to escape punishment from a person outside one's kinship was a 'good' effort. At school, there were no half-measures; we were all expected to be honest pupils. Was I to accept the school standards for the sake of being able to stay here, away from my early playmates?

I had done, while a child at home, what my parents had asked me to do. But there was never much worry if the work was not finished or if it was badly done. Somebody would complete or perfect it. At school it was different. The teachers expected me to do my work carefully, quickly, and accurately. If it was badly done I would be punished—either flogged, detained at school, or given a number of bricks to make. If the work was well done, on the other hand, I would be praised. On a number of occasions I was given prizes for good performance. Most of my former playmates, who could not fit into this new scheme of things, went back to the country and home life for good. The discipline of our parents, their rewards (if any) and their punishments, had formed in us no strong motives for doing our best, which was what all the formalities of the school were aimed at.

It was at school that I first realized the educative value of play. At home we had always loved to play, but to my mother, as to most parents then, it was a waste of time. She only tolerated it when it suited her convenience for us to play. Although those teachers who taught us for the first four years were not of 'trained calibre', I realized that they encouraged my efforts. I could see myself being guided into new undertakings and being encouraged to take leadership amongst my classmates.

Again, at home I had not been given a chance to care for and look after a bit of property that I could really call 'mine.' At school I found I possessed a set of articles which for a period were mine. I had to begin afresh learning how to respect not only my things, but those that belonged to my classmates and to the school as a whole. This strange concept of individual ownership introduced a new element in my experience. The school required that the individual pupil should pay for any article lost while in his possession. Well I remember when once I lost a pen-holder costing twenty-five cents. I knew that my home could not provide me with the twenty-five cents. Money was a new idea to all of us anyway. Wouldn't the easiest way be to steal my neighbour's pen and call it mine? The home, as I have said, had offered me no clear-cut basis for self-regard, no strong ideals for controlling temptation such as this. I was surprised to find myself deciding to tell the teacher what had happened, and still more surprised when he in turn gave me another pen-holder.

Above all, the school, naturally, insisted upon hygiene—high standards of bodily cleanliness and orderliness. I have said earlier that in these matters, my home was far from being helpful. Without individual ownership and a responsibility for property in the early years, I had developed no sense of orderliness. Besides, in the home in which I grew up cleanliness was not practised. As I look back on it now, my home made very little attempt to train me in matters of cleanliness, in body or in other things. Judging from what I remember of myself and my sister, our hair was rarely cut or washed, for to do this, adults believed, was to invite disease. My parents did not think of combing the hair. For to start with they had no combs and, secondly, it would only have added to other numerous and 'more important' duties. Later in my life, copying the practice from other youngsters, I found myself combing my hair. Perhaps the parents regarded combing, if they thought of it at all, as a thing for later years only to be performed by the child himself. I remember seeing my parents clean their own teeth, cut their own nails, and wash their own faces. But they never extended these practices to include me or my sister. As a nurse, and in conjunction with other young nurses, I took it upon myself from time to time to go to the river to bathe myself and my sister as well. But I was unable to cut my own nails because the blade I tried to use was meant for harvesting millet.

For us, as children, clothes were unheard of. At night I slept at my grandfather's house on a skin folded in two halves so that, while one half was spread on the floor, I would cover myself with the other half. This skin was never cleaned. It was thought that washing it would make the skin too thin for the cool Idakho nights. The floor on which it was spread harboured fleas, lice, and jiggers. I was a victim of these parasites for a very long time.

In some homes where I visited with my playmates, I could see that parents insisted on our washing our hands before we started eating. In others, mothers insisted that we wash the utensils we used before leaving the home. Elsewhere, too, I saw mothers actually sweeping the floor after we had used it for eating. In such homes I saw that the parents had the habit of trying to keep things in order in the house. But such 'orderly' homes were few and were mainly influenced by missionaries.

I had grown up in a home where religious practices were very much influenced by strong belief in witchcraft and magic. I had taken part in some of the magical rites connected with the burial of heroes and heroines. I had participated in sacrificial ceremonies and festivities carried on for various reasons and covering various cases. My parents were not converts to any of the foreign missions, although they sympathized with the Roman Catholics. And yet here I was, attending a Christian school with strong traditional teaching. Here again the school—and I—had to begin afresh.

It was not an easy matter for me to remain in school. I should not have stayed had it not been for the persuasion of my early teachers. My father objected firmly, partly because he had no money to pay my school fees but mainly because he wanted me to carry on with the economic activities of the home. Secondly, my own playmates who had found it intolerable to continue at school were insistent on getting me out. Thirdly, there were my own fears of the new environment: How should I get clothes for the uniform required by the school? How should I get soap for bathing? How should I raise the fees? What would the classroom work involve? Would I be able to do it? Would I be accepted by these other pupils? Would my father punish me for remaining at school? Would my own playmates disown me when I went back to them after school?

Though as a child I could not put all of this into words, I was afraid in fact of being 'in two different worlds, with two different sets of values'. I wonder if I even now have got over this fear.

Despite all these doubts my teachers made me feel that there was something intrinsically valuable about remaining at school. And so, alone out of the village, I walked each morning a distance of ten miles to pursue further schooling.

9.

Thoughts on Adolescents

In Buluyia the biggest event in the period of adolescence is the traditional circumcision with its ceremonies and practices, reminding the youth that he is about to enter manhood, physically, mentally, and in every other way. Any time after these rituals are performed, the youngster may generally proceed to press his parents for marriage. The fact that he gets married, though, does not mean he becomes independent of his parents. I knew of a couple who have remained attached to the parents and completely dependent on them for ten years. In such cases, the young couple will normally live on a part of the parents' land, sharing the use of the home property until it is officially divided among the sons of the family. For example, although I am married and have a family, my father does not regard me and my household as independent of him. He considers me still under his authority and will do so until such time as he divides his property (mainly land) among the three of his sons.

Through the adolescent years the boy is supposed to be trained to become a good citizen of the tribe and, later, a good parent. Already some of his youthful energy will have been used in building his own house, just in front of his father's. In some families too, more frequently these days than when I was a boy, an adolescent is given his own plot or *shamba* to look after and raise crops from. Such harvest as he may reap will belong to the family. Should he want to sell part of it, in order to raise money for his own use, he must first seek the permission of his parents. It is believed, and hoped, that through proper training the boy will continue, as he advances in years, to take an active part in the life of the tribe.

The Western impact, however, is making young persons prematurely independent of their parents, causing the educated adolescents to disregard those tribal customs which traditionally have been passed on from one generation to the next. Modern youth—myself included—find these customs increasingly incompatible with the desired way of life. Many young people are tending to 'flee' the tribe altogether and go to the towns. In my own case, the energies typical of adolescence were constructively channelled at school. I have moved on through

secondary and higher education with a definite aim. My
school days culminated in my being admitted to Makerere
University College in January of 1953, in order to pursue a
Higher Arts Course leading to a Diploma Course in Education.
I completed the course successfully in December 1956, and was
employed as a teacher at Kapsabet High School the following
year.

My father objected to this posting, arguing that it put me in a
non-Luyia tribe and a tribe—the Nandi—which has been a traditional enemy of the Luyia. He also maintained that since Kapsabet
is a town (it is actually a township) I too would probably be
'lost'. His objections never reached the Government, of course;
so I taught at Kapsabet for four years, going home on vacations
to help with the family farm work. All this time, even after
I was married, there was continued agitation for me to return
to Buluyia; so in 1961 I moved to Kyavakali High School in
Maragoli. Later that year I was transferred to Kaimosi Teacher
Training College from where, by now a married man and the
father of two young children, I decided to come back for further
education here at Makerere in July of 1963, leaving my family
at Kaimosi where my wife was on the College staff.

But what about the youngsters of my earlier play group who
never went to school? Any such youth has had almost no alternative but to follow the advice of his parents in choosing a job
or occupation; there was no choice except to take up the occupation in which the father or perhaps a close relative was engaged.
The adolescent at home learned gradually from his father the
traditional ways of cultivation, say, of pottery-making, crafts-
manship, fishing, hunting, building. If I had not gone to school—
and the chances were close, it will be remembered—I would
probably have become a craftsman, since my paternal uncle's
occupation was to make stools and *miikho*, used for preparing
the flour *bushuma*. Besides, as a boy I was always interested in
crafts. Failing this line, I should have been either a fisherman or
a land-cultivator, because my father was both.

Except for those who are hampered by lack of money for
school fees, most youths in Idakho today do go to school. Depending on the type of home from which they come, a few of them
will still seek the advice of their parents as to which job they
should decide to train for. There are others who seek the advice
of their teachers, first because of the closer contact many

students have with them, and secondly because they know the
teachers are apt to be less traditional in their outlook. At any
rate, the influence of teachers in our community has convinced
many parents and young people that teaching is a very respectable
and profitable profession. When Idakho youth seek the advice
of their parents today as to which jobs they should take up after
school, they are frequently told to join the teaching ranks.

But there are other considerations. Putting aside the fact that
teaching would put them closer to their communities and
kinsfolk, most adolescents consider first those jobs in which
there is prestige for them as educated men or women, in which
chances of promotion are bright, and above all, in which there
is the possibility of making money. This is a powerful factor in
young men's decisions whenever alternatives are available. I
recently talked with three former students whom I personally
had implored to become teachers, and whose parents, I know,
were anxious that they should become teachers. After School
Certificate, however, they decided to join a large oil firm,
where they now hold responsible posts. They were conscious
of the fact that in joining this business firm, they were going
against the wishes of their teachers as well as their parents. Such
conflict was outweighed, realistically enough, by the fact that
the openings in the business carried salaries several times higher
than any teaching positions for which they perhaps could ever
qualify.

Of the young people who attend school but do not obtain
jobs, most go reluctantly back to till the land. If they do not
raise enough money to satisfy them—and many of them do not—
they go into the towns and, in most instances finding no job
and therefore no money, they turn to wrong means of raising
money—car stealing, robbing, house-breaking—all too often
turning out to be among the worst citizens in the country.
Needless to say, this is a great disappointment and worry to
their parents.

There is mounting concern on the part of the older generation
also regarding the sex activities of the young. It is widely
realized that young people today tend to indulge in excessive
romantic behaviour and premarital sexual relationships much
more freely than heretofore. Such practices were firmly forbidden
in the days of my youth. It was then considered absolutely
shameful for a girl to have premarital children. Such a girl
would be thrown out of the family, perhaps sent to stay with

some distant relative, and the offender would be required to pay heavy compensation in accordance with tribal law.

The present numerous premarital'pregnancies are commonly attributed to co-educational schools, where girls, it is said, are exposed to immoral attitudes, and from which both boys and girls go to towns and indulge in practices wholly unacceptable to parents. In these towns, as already said, they seek employment; but they also take to such town ways as have made quite a number of boys lose the wish for marriage completely. The girls become exposed to some irresponsible young men and, being away from their parents' watchful care, may often fall easy victims of these men whose intentions are not to get married. As a result of this, the educated as well as the illiterate parents are fearful of sending their daughters to school if by being educated, the girls stand a greater chance of ending up in prostitute quarters or suffering a similar fate in the towns. That other factors, including at times the unbending attitudes of the parents themselves, may also enter the situation, does not seem to diminish the blame which the Baluyia generally choose to put on the schools.

Traditionally, it was the father who 'fixed' a boy to a particular girl, because the conduct and behaviour of such girl would already be thought to be acceptable to the parents of the boy. In days gone by, the two young people would never meet until they were actually married. Thus, in Buluyia, the parents decided whom their children should marry. The parents did not expect, once their decision was made, that there would be any challenging of it. Nor did they realize that their decision could possibly lead to future conflict in the home of their making.

Western culture, however, has once again changed the order of things. Since with education has come the urge for them to be independent of their parents, more and more young people are coming to choose their own nuptial partners. Even so, there are fathers who still wish to exercise their right to advise and be heeded, arguing that the modern youth selects a partner 'more for externals like beauty and dress than for good upbringing, manners and ability to work hard in the *shambas*'.

When I made my choice in 1954, my father began intensive 'research' through his friends in the area and several remote relatives, just to discover what sort of upbringing my chosen partner had had. By the time we got married a few years later, he knew well that my wife would be acceptable to him and his kinsfolk. He complained only that I had not sought his permission for marriage in advance.

To repeat, the youth of my tribe are traditionally tied to the care of their parents for a long time. Neither marriage, school-leaving, employment, nor wage earning has convinced my father that I am, or should be, independent of him. Out of a sense of filial duty and, after all, an appreciation of what my sincere, hard-working parents had given the child Lijembe as best they knew, I have not chosen to sever these ties. This is true, it would seem, of only the minority of educated Baluyia. I could cite case after case of young men who, disclaiming their parents' authority, flee from the home just as soon as their school days are over. Fortunate employment affords many of them completely independent living, providing ample means with which to maintain themselves and later their young families, away from and without assistance from the tribal home. Some of these, feeling an obligation to help support their old parents in line with tradition, send home a certain amount of money each month and, in pride, let that be their only contact with their tribal past. They may add, as the rest of us do, school fees for their young brothers and sisters.

Thus, the increasing adoption of 'foreign' culture by the young people, to the neglect of many aspects of the old tribal culture, is of growing concern to their elders. The old skills of wood-carving among the Abidakho, for example, pottery-making among the Abagoli, blacksmithing among the Abisukha, and traditional education throughout the tribe, are all being surrendered to Western culture, largely acquired from our European-type schools, from expanding opportunities for travel, and from life in the towns. There seems to be little chance of persuading adolescents of Buluyia, educated or uneducated, to carry on these traditional crafts so essential to the culture of our parents and grandparents. Indeed, it seems probable that our youngsters will gradually lose whatever sense of tribal cultural identity they may still have retained.

Again, parents in the location and throughout the tribe blame all of this directly on the schools and the teachers who, they insist, are 'spoiling' their sons. Since the child enters school very early in life—at the age of seven or even earlier—there is very little chance that he will have learned by that age to appreci-ate anything of his tribal ways, or have had sufficient time, before the intensive process of Europeanization begins, to acquire the basic principles of his own culture. As a result, he looks for a white-collar job after school, because that is the job of the educated Westerner whom he probably has admired, respected, or at least envied, for a long time.

But blaming the schools, even when justified, is neither an answer nor a solution to the problem. The East African countries are all independent now. Africans more and more are moving into positions of leadership, in education as well as in other branches of government. Professor S. H. Ominde, for example, has submitted to the Government a Report of his Commission of Enquiry, appointed in December 1963 to undertake an exhaustive enquiry into all aspects of education in Kenya. From the Commission's findings and recommendations, the Government is attempting to formulate a system of education which will effectively respond to the country's rapidly changing conditions. We ourselves then, Africans in the main, are having to decide what we shall teach our children and youth about the past, the present, and the future, and through what means. The changes may not be as rapid as some would wish, nor as thoroughgoing. Our African leaders themselves have been educated in the very schools that are now being blamed, and are proud of that education; in large measure it has put them where they are. I, too, have learned and taught in such schools. The important point for us Africans now is that, from here on, the responsibility lies with ourselves.

10.

The Forces of Change

The changes just referred to seem to be pushing us, whether we like it or not, on to the broader world scene. Marketing agreements at every level affect us greatly. This means that our society is coming to function as a cash or money economy.

The money economy, with its impact on our traditional structure, is introducing changes in several important directions. It has led a growing proportion of the young of Abaluyia to look for employment outside their own villages, mainly in urban areas. Most of these are young men who, if they are married and have families, leave their children under the care of their wives or their grandparents. Such children grow up without close contact with the father—earlier true of only the youngest children, and for a different reason—and therefore, without any full notion of parental relationships and co-operation. Not only is this likely to affect their own parenthood in future, but the absence of these young men from the village society has helped to disrupt further our tribal customs and traditions. True, the towns have the advantage of being popular among the young educated persons, and of securing for the family a cash income. But it is also important to repeat that while in towns some of these young Abaluyia fall victim, like any other townsmen, to the bad side of town life. First, they are not adequately prepared for town life. And secondly, they are away from the parents on whose authority and judgement they have depended for a long time.

A second main change introduced by the money economy has to do with the Western concept of formal education which is set up to enable an individual to earn his own living. Because a young person is educated, earns his salary and probably lives away from his parents, he becomes financially independent. In so doing, he acquires new customs and ways of thinking. He begins questioning and in most cases disagreeing with his older beliefs. In these circumstances, the parents' insistence on obedience is of little avail and punishment carries no meaning. Village life, and especially the role of the father in a family, is in a state of uncertainty throughout the whole of Buluyia, as the father's parental authority over his children steadily diminishes.

Another change is that the fruits of technological advancement which, as in other parts of the world, have affected Kenya over the years, are at the door of every educated Muluyia. Comfortable furniture, improved cooking and eating facilities are becoming common. Radios, transistor or otherwise, and newspapers are in a growing number of homes. Travel for many youngsters is done on bicycles. Children in some town homes have these as toys, in fact. Because a good number of women are able to earn their own living and can therefore afford to be financially independent, they are no longer submissive as in the past. Many of them are aggressively claiming recognition along with the men in the society. Their dress, at least for those who can afford it, is comparable to that of women in the West.

An influential group of economically advanced Baluyia, chiefly traders, teachers, administrators and progressive farmers, have abandoned the traditional type of dwelling in favour of European-type houses, frequently built of bricks with corrugated-iron roofs. The chief problems in this type of house still centre on water and light. But schemes are under way to provide more homes with tap water. Before long, too, as things are going, electricity will be in use not only in Kakamega town, but also in the neighbouring countryside. Such permanent homes will in due course be served by these mains, as the demand for electric light and other related conveniences increases.

Agriculture, too, is undergoing changes. Attempts have been made to improve the production of our chief crops, bananas, sorghum and maize. Today as one travels through Idakho, one sees hybrid maize being grown. New cash crops include coffee and tea, both of these grown on the smallholder basis. It looks as if, eventually, they will be cultivated on the new co-operative plan. The Kenya Government has set up statutory Marketing Boards through which agricultural products are to be controlled.

To help our economic advancement, the Government has named four projects to be established in Buluyia as soon as possible. Plans for a paper factory at Broderick Falls in the Bungoma County, and for a sugar factory at Mumias, in Busia, are being widely discussed. A cassava factory is planned for the Kakamega County, at Butere. And as soon as Kakamega township is served by electricity, the now defunct Rosterman gold-mines are expected to reopen. All of these will bring new patterns and new scope for employment for Baluyia men and women, and the higher standards of living that steady, well-paid employment makes possible.

Politically, a large section of the Abaluyia once belonged to the Kenya African Democratic Union which opposed the present ruling Kenya African National Union. When KADU went into voluntary dissolution a couple of years ago Kenya became a one-party state. The Abaluyia are now solidly behind the present Government headed by H.E. Mzee Jomo Kenyatta.

Thus, political, social and economic changes are great and rapid. They have necessitated a re-examination of our pre-independence educational structure and the formulation of a new one commensurate with our present and future needs. Hence the Ominde Education Commission of 1963, already referred to. These forces of change necessarily affect the way we are going to bring up our children, if they are to be capable not only of regenerating the location and tribal values, but also of playing their full and effective part in all aspects of national life, keeping close, as Abaluyia, to the rest of Kenya and to the world at large. True it is that our children today are born and bred in an unsettled environment. But I believe the prevalent forces of change are, or can be channelled to be, for the better. Growing up in Idakho today should mean a better life ahead.

11.

On Being a Modern Parent

I should like now to consider the role, including my own, of Idakho parents today. Let me say first that owing to the forces just described there have been changes throughout the tribe, though mainly among the educated, in the attitudes towards parenthood generally.

While in the past the more children there were in a Baluyia family, the more highly respected the parents were in the society, today a small but growing number of parents are thinking in terms of smaller families. The case for many children to increase a family's work-force is gradually losing ground as employment patterns change and parents realize how expensive it is to care for large families in modern times. Neither do so many parents think, as in the past, of girls primarily as a source of wealth from bride price. A father with a large family, without reasonable sources of wealth to educate and to care for them adequately, is beginning to lose favour with the rest of the society.

Changes related to pregnancy and childbirth are also taking place. Now, as never in the past, there are expectant mothers who no longer undertake strenuous work right up to childbirth. Through increased medical care they are learning that to do so may affect the position of the child in the womb, and perhaps cause other serious complications. Husbands with some elementary education have become aware of the advantage of allowing their wives to have more rest during pregnancy. These women also are talking more freely, which was once taboo, about conception, pregnancy and childbirth, not only among themselves, but with their husbands and, above all, with physicians and nurses. Many expectant mothers in or near the towns make an effort to visit a hospital or a health centre for pre- and later, postnatal examinations. In fact, there is pressure on the Government by the educated group of mothers to provide classes for expectant mothers especially where they can receive help from experts. Certainly the children of modern parents will be born at a maternity home or hospital since, in addition to services there being free, the Government now requires that all children be registered and that the registration certificate bear the name of the place of birth and the medical staff in attendance. In my own case, our three young children were born at a hospital and have certificates of birth, documents which the parents of neither their mother nor myself would have reason to know when we were born in the thirties.

These new requirements mean, in effect, that both parents will have to make early preparations for the arrival of the child, however contrary to tribal tradition. For example, they have to buy, in advance, articles of clothing adequate for the baby's needs. This practice has long been taboo in the tribe, of course, for fear of causing the child's death. The expectant mother, as has been said, will have to make frequent visits to the clinic and consult other experts. She will have to read books on child care, securing information about the right diet and conditions of rest. The father, too, will have to assume a different role from formerly, learning to create a comfortable, restful atmosphere for the mother both before and after delivery. Since our children must have a fair start in life, these things are imperative.

Certain rituals and practices connected with traditional child rearing among the Baluyia have long been losing ground, as previous pages indicate. The removal of the lower front teeth, to which I as a child was subjected, is no longer practised. Circumcision, in a growing number of cases, is performed at a hospital. Above all, fathers now take a keener interest in children, especially babies, than ever before. Fathers as well as mothers now spend more time with all of their children, who are coming to be not only seen but also heard. Among some families children are brought into social gatherings of various kinds, formerly prohibited to them, and are allowed to share these occasions with adults.

It isn't always easy for modern parents to change from the old ways. My wife and I, for example, are trying to bring up our children in line with what Western books on child-rearing and child development advise. At the same time we wonder at the wisdom of thus trying to fit them into a life based on the Western culture when in actual fact a good proportion of their time as children will be lived with other children in the traditional Luyia society. This tends to create a feeling of insecurity in the parents—and perhaps in the children.

While we are able to buy for our children, for example, the toys that are essential to their play, their little cousins in the villages continue to play in the traditional manner, much as we did. Often, because they are unaccustomed to the modern ones, the cousins will become destructive with our children's toys when we happen to go there for a stay. Similarly we supplied our children with Western food in a Western manner in their early stages. Since that time they have also been introduced to the local food and the traditional way of eating it. Thus the whole process of learning to eat becomes complicated for them. Our children have to learn that there are certain times and places—and foods—when spoons are used for eating; others when knives and forks are the proper instruments; still others—as when eating the traditional *bushuma* or maize-meal—when the use of the hands only is the acceptable way. They must drink water from glasses at one moment and from traditional containers at other times.

Another typical instance can be cited. In naming our three children, we decided to differ from the customary Luyia practice. My children have taken my name, Lijembe, as a surname, in addition to their Christian names. From the traditional tribal standpoint this has caused difficulties in at least two ways. First, Baluyia daughters have always taken some woman's name. Hence our fellow villagers object to the fact that our two little daughters, Pamela and Matilda, are also called Lijembe. The objection to our son Vincent's being called by my name is that a son, as indicated in earlier pages, is supposed to take on the name of an important man of the tribe, whose death occurred just before the baby's birth. Secondly, when village visitors want to refer to our children by name in my presence, they find it difficult, if not embarrassing, to use the name Lijembe for all of us. Western tradition says that in such an instance Christian names should be used, but among the Idakho villagers, the custom is to preserve the use of Christian names for adults only. When my father visits us and plays with the children, as he loves to do, he rarely calls them by name. It is not within his experience or nature to refer to his grandchildren by his son's name. Neither would he refer to them by their Christian names.

To try to avoid such difficult situations by isolating ourselves and our children from the village life is a solution we feel that we cannot afford, the traditional ties between us and our parents being still so strong. On the face of things, in fact, this is a simple and almost unimportant matter, as are the others just described. Yet each is the sort of thing that causes confusion and disappointment to the elders, and can set in motion feelings of indecision on the part of modern parents trying to rear our children in 'the valley between'. It is good that the children at least, because they *are* children, are far more flexible in these situations than we are.

Another matter of greater concern is that since, to repeat, many educated mothers have sought employment in office work, teaching, nursing, etc., there is a clear falling off of breast-feeding among babies and a steady increase in the cases of early weaning. Although early weaning and bottle-feeding are preferred by working mothers, partly from necessity, and partly perhaps because these devices help the mothers to regain their 'natural' size and shape quickly, Dr. D. B. Jelliffe sounds a warning to modern parents: 'Bottle-feeding is harmful nutritionally and from the point of view of infection,' he told us. 'And it is the antithesis of the close mother-child relationship of the traditional village.' In these circumstances, what do modern parents do? They cannot set the clock back, but must be confident and hopeful, making decisions on the basis of the best modern knowledge available and adapting it as wisely as they can to the realities of their own situation.

As pointed out previously, in most modern homes today there will most likely be found a radio, books for adults and some for children perhaps, and newspapers. Also the children will have a collection of toys, in many cases even bicycles or tricyles. The parents now have cars. Such children will have a better chance of broadening their knowledge than we their parents did as children. Also, because in modern homes children are more free to talk with adults and ask questions, they should be able to think more clearly, to express their ideas, to seek to find out. They will also tend to be less fearful of strangers than we were taught to be. With their parents as examples, they too will read books, newspapers, and other literature. They will hear adult conversations and, no doubt, political discussions. These incentives will encourage the children's being sent to school much earlier than has been the case before. For instance, although I went to school at the age of ten, my son has joined primary school at the age of five, having spent a year in nursery school.

It is imperative that when our children grow up to become adults, they should have among other things a clear sense of balance. We recognize that the ties of traditional village life and kinship are still very strong, and that as cultural changes take place, there will be a case for future generations to retain, at least in part, those aspects of our culture that are worth keeping. We recognize, too, that the schools and other educational institutions have, as everywhere else, to assist the future Abidakho to appreciate what is good in both tribal and Western cultures, and that the future may discover some things better than either. To be able to help our children to achieve this appreciation, today's parents will need to be critical of the steps we take in the process of child rearing. Being educated ourselves, we hold positions of leadership in the society, and must act accordingly. Careful application of Western methods of health and childcare, and critical retention of what is good in traditional methods, can help us modern parents to create the sense of balance in our children, enabling the future generation to work out, from the two cultures, a way of life more appropriate than either one of these, in line with what the people of Idakho, of Buluyia, and of Kenya will be wanting most.

AT HOME IN THE VILLAGE:

Growing Up in Acholi

by
Anna Apoko

1.

Village Birthplace

The Acholi people live in the north of Uganda. To the west of the District, the River Nile marks their boundary with the West Nile District. To the east there lies Karamoja, to the south Lango District; to the north, the boundary of the Sudan cuts across, leaving some of the Acholi in Sudan.

The Acholi people were originally divided into several chiefdoms. The most important of these were Payira, Patiko, Puranga, and Koich, my own chiefdom with which I am mainly concerned. Each chiefdom has many clans and each clan has many families. Groups of families, who are very often related to one another, live together in a village. The population of a village often drinks from the same well, and groups all the crops in the same place every year. A village with many people can also have a dancing field, with a high pole in the centre for the drum. (Acholi dancers have been famous throughout Uganda for many years.) People living in the same village have a lot in common. When the rainy season approaches, the men often gather together and go to open one another's new cotton, simsim, groundnut or millet fields in turn. This makes digging easier and more enjoyable than if one man tries to work alone on his field. The man whose new cotton field is to be opened always arranges a big beer party for the workers. The women also work in groups, helping one another weed in their gardens.

Within each village family in Acholi, there is a strict division of labour between the father and the mother, or husband and wife. The father or husband is the head of the family. He has the decisive voice on all matters concerning the family. Acholi people follow the patrilineal system of inheritance. Every father makes it a point to train his son to become a strong-willed man, who cannot be dominated by a woman. The husband's work is the cutting of wood for building a house and the actual building of the house. The wife's work is to cut grass for thatching the roof. The man also digs the field and sows the seed, but it is the work of the woman to keep the garden clear of weeds and to harvest the crops like millet, simsim, peas and beans. All domestic work concerned with cooking is the work of the woman. It is a disgrace for a grown up man or even a boy to go to the well and carry water. That is the work of a woman. Grinding is also the work of a woman; no man in Acholi must grind. Anything concerned with babies and young children is a woman's work.

A man who has so many acres of cotton, millet, and simsim, so many grain stores full of millet, simsim, and peas, who has so many cows or goats; a man whose houses are big and strong; a man who is brave in hunting and fighting—is considered a good and successful man in rural Acholi and is respected by society. A lot of songs are often composed, especially by women, for such men. For example, this one:

> *Odai we ye,*
> *Odai latin acel pire tek,*
> *Obutu kicel long gang oling tik.*

> Our Odai,
> The only great one.
> He was absent for a day
>   and the house went to pieces.

Likewise, a woman whose house is well smeared with black soil and kept clean; who has a lot of food in her home; who cooks and gives generously to visitors (according to the Acholi custom requiring the wife to cook or at least give food to any visitor who comes at any time); a woman whose gardens are well kept; who mixes freely and happily with other women in the village; and who has children—is considered a good woman. Such a woman can be called to join a meeting of village elders to give some talks and advice. Very often such things as this are said about her: *Dako pa Okot dako ki cumun. Dako man minne opwongo ada*. 'Mrs. Okot is a woman and a half. She must have had really good training from her mother.'

Such are the Acholi's ideal people, those who are liked and valued by the whole community. The aim of traditional education or of bringing up children in Acholi is to produce such citizens. People take great care to see that children are given all the necessary training in order that they will be hard-working and useful men and women in the society; men and women who will not have to starve because they cannot cultivate for themselves. Great attention is paid to all aspects of children's 'moral' development. They must learn to obey those who are older than they are. A boy, particularly, has to grow up obeying his father's brothers, who are just as important and influential to him as is his own father. He must respect his mother's brothers, who may curse him and cause ill luck for him if he disrespects them. He must also grow up in close contact with the gods of his grandfathers and must know how to keep *abila*, the shrine.

Everybody who is closely related to the child takes part in, and contributes, towards the child's education. Uncles, aunts stepmothers, elder brothers and sisters, all are members of staff. Teaching takes place through teasing (*ngala*), songs, educative stories (*ododo*) and practical work.

2.

A Baby is Welcomed

Every married couple in Acholi wants to have children; they are invaluable for many reasons. Children are useful in the home. A woman who has daughters or even one daughter, from five years old upwards, is greatly relieved and helped in her daily household duties. Children help with work on the farm. In the old days, before the coming of school education, boys were very useful in that whenever a village went out hunting, a man who had many sons was sure to have a lot of meat brought home for him. Children are helpful for support in old age. An old man who is unable to dig and grow food is very often given food by his sons' wives. This is where sons are more valuable than the daughters who by this time are married and living with their husbands in another clan. Sons are very import-ant, too, because they uphold the family line. All married couples in rural Acholi, therefore, want to have as many children as they can possibly have. Nobody ever stops to think about family planning. Even with the coming of school education, which involves paying school fees, parents would rather go without clothes, sugar, or soap in order to save money for school fees than to cut down the number of children they produce. If a man cannot afford to educate all his children, the girls have to stay at home while the boys go to school.

To have no child is the most serious misfortune one can have. A barren woman suffers a great deal. She is scolded and looked down upon by the husband. His mother and father, brothers and sisters, all join up in despising her. They talk loudly and openly, regretting that they ever wasted so many cattle or so much money on him for marrying a barren woman. Very often such a woman is either sent away, divorced—and the bride-price received back and used for marrying another wife—or, if the man can afford it, he marries another woman as well. Poly-gamy is common in Acholi and is encouraged by the tribal law.

Pregnancy is always a very pleasant occasion in an Acholi village. The woman feels happy about it because at last she has proved herself worthy. Most women keep it a secret, telling their husbands only. If it is the first pregnancy there is always some kind of ceremony which the woman has to undergo.

The ceremony differs from clan to clan. In my clan, a pregnant young woman is given *ceno*, a string skirt, to wear for the whole day. Nothing in the way of preparation for the expected baby is to be made before the baby is born. This would bring ill luck to the mother, who might die in childbirth or give birth to a dead child.

When a pregnant woman begins labour, she sends for an older and more experienced woman to come and help her, either her mother or her husband's mother. No one else is considered reliable. Other women, it is feared, can do evil things—take a drop of the mother's blood, for example, and bury it in a hole near a white ant-hill. This will stop the mother from having any more children. A certain woman near my home was brought before the elders by a woman neighbour who suspected she was late in conceiving her second baby because the first woman, who had helped her in the previous birth, had done something evil to her.

The way in which a baby comes out during birth also matters. A baby who comes out head first in the normal way is called by any name. One who comes out legs first is named *Adoc* if it is a girl, and *Odoc* if he is a boy. A baby who comes out face downward is called *Auma* if a girl, and *Uma* if a boy. The first twin is called *Apiyo* if a girl, *Opiyo* if a boy; and the second twin *Acen* if a girl and *Ocen* if a boy. The umbilical cord of any such child is very carefully buried in a pot in a known place, from which it can be dug out if there is trouble with the child's health later on.

For three days if the newborn is a boy, and four if the newborn is a girl, the mother and the baby are kept strictly inside the house. Nobody from outside the home is allowed to enter, not even a relative. It is believed that if people enter the house they can hurt the baby's eyes or make the baby appear small and unhealthy. This rule is also a precaution against anybody who might come with the intention of preventing the mother from having any more children. During these three or four days the mother must eat but little food, not too much because her stomach is still delicate. She is not allowed to eat salt with her food. The person looking after the mother cooks for her some *mala kwang*, a sour green vegetable which is supposed to be very good for the stimulation of milk flow. This is also eaten without salt during the first three or four days.

On the third or fourth day, depending on the sex, the baby

is brought out early in the morning. Beans or cow peas are cooked specially for that occasion. They are eaten out in the courtyard under the warm morning sun. Anybody, including relatives, may come now and give a name to the young baby. Apart from the natural names already mentioned—*Adoc, Auma, Apiyo*, and so on—any name suggested must be supported by good reasons and explanations. All the names in my clan have meanings attached to them. The names *Angom, Abur*, or *Alobo*, if they are for girls, and *Ongom, Obur*, or *Olobo*, if they are for boys, suggest sorrow. They mean that the mother has previously given birth to several children who died. The words *Lobo* and *Ngom* mean earth, and *Bur* means hole or a grave. Through these names the mother says that this child has just come temporarily; later it will go to the earth. After the naming of the child the mother is taken to the well to fetch some water. From that time onwards she is expected to carry on her normal house duties.

3.

The Feeding and Care of Children

Feeding a child at the breast is the common practice in Acholi. All village mothers breast-feed their babies. There is no regular time for feeding babies. Whenever a baby cries, it is given the breast. If a mother is unable to breast-feed her baby, or if she dies, usually some suckling mother takes over and feeds the two babies together as if they were twins. Otherwise the baby may be fed on cow's milk.

As soon as a mother has given birth to her baby, if she does not have older children of her own, she looks around among her relatives for *lapidi*, a selected young child, preferably a girl from six to ten years old, to act as the baby's 'nurse.' During a recent vacation I met a woman who was once my classmate; she had come sixty-five miles from where she was living with her husband, back to her father's home, looking for *lapidi*. She found a little girl, five years old, who went back with her.

The very young baby, from one to three months old, is tied on *lapidi's* back. *Lapidi*, carrying the baby in this way, goes with the mother to the field where she may be working for most of the day. If the baby wakes up from its sleep and begins to cry, the mother unties it from the child's back and breast-feeds it. By the time the baby is four months old, it may be left at home with *lapidi*, who again follows after the mother as soon as the baby is hungry and begins to cry. Nurses have many lullaby songs which they sing when the babies cry. For example, this:

> *Latin kok ngo?*
> *Meni otedo aluri ki kwon.*
>
> Baby, why do you cry?
> Your mother has cooked a fowl and some millet.

Sometimes the nurse becomes so tired, poor child, that she may begin wearily singing a song about the mother of the child, such as: *Min latin do tedo dyerwor.* . . . 'The child's mother cooks so late in the night.' If the mother has the food nearly ready she calls, 'Bring me my baby! Do not break its back!' But when she realizes that she has not yet cooked the millet, she will say to *lapidi*, 'Take the baby and play with it, out of my sight!' If the baby goes on crying, the nurse will again tie it on her back and follow the mother about the house.

I was *lapidi* for my little cousin for about a year. How I loved that baby! I wanted to be with him all the time. Perhaps this was because I had requested to be *lapidi*. The duty had not been forced on me. By the time the baby was able to walk well and firmly, and another little girl cousin was old enough to be his nurse, I had to give him up so that I could go to school.

A mother who does not have *lapidi* is bound to carry her baby about wherever she goes and whatever she does. Such mothers often sing this lullaby to their babies:

> *Nynyu ka ikok ngo?*
> *Lapidi meri peke.*
> *Onyu ling.*
> *Lapidi meri obeno.*

> Why do you cry, my baby?
> You have no *lapidi*?
> *Obeno* is your nurse.
> Keep quiet, baby, you have no nurse.

Thus *lapidi* is the second mother to the baby; and there are some babies who are fonder of their *lapidi* than of their own mothers.

Only in the homes of rich educated parents are babies fed on cow's milk, in addition to breast milk. The Acholi are not pastoral people; and milk is scarce and expensive. An ordinary family in the village, unless they have cows of their own, cannot afford to use milk. So from birth to seven months the baby is fed on breast milk alone. After that the child begins to take solid food, usually millet porridge, which the mother instructs the nurse to make for the child in her absence. The baby is also fed on roasted ground simsim or groundnuts, of which, incidentally, children are very fond. By the time the baby is one year old, he can eat in small quantities whatever adults eat.

Weaning takes place as soon as the mother discovers a new pregnancy. At this time the milk is said to be bad for the child. Before this, most women see no reason for weaning. Unless they are pregnant, they usually go on breast-feeding their babies until long after the babies can walk or run. Some lastborn children are known to suck for four or five years, until they leave off voluntarily as a result of other people's scornful words.

Irii icak toki golle. 'If you suck for a long time you develop a hole at the back of your head.' This hole is supposed to be caused by constant bending of the head in order to reach the breast.

Because they lose their favourite food and their mother's close attention and love in the same abrupt process, weaning can be the most painful experience of childhood for many children. Often Acholi mothers will wean their babies by putting bitter herbs or hot pepper on to the nipples. This discourages the child from sucking. Some mothers wean the children by going away on a visit, staying for two or three days so that the baby will become accustomed to doing without breast milk. Weaned children are fed on whatever adults eat, with peas, beans, meat, groundnuts and simsim as their favourite foods. If a mother roasts groundnuts or simsim and begins grinding it, she always gives some of it to the young children to eat. This is one of the reasons, perhaps, why Acholi children do not seem to suffer from malnutrition, as much as do children in Buganda, for instance.

At meal time all the children eat with the mother, sitting on the kitchen floor, while the father eats alone. It is common in the villages to find a group of two or three families eating together, each woman having cooked two separate dishes, one for the men and one for the women and children. If there are a large number of children, one separate dish can be served to the children only. The two or three men, heads of the different families, will sit together near a fire outside or inside a house. They put each woman's dish in their midst and eat them in turn.

It is considered very important that when children are eating, they sit up straight, without supporting themselves on the arm. This leaning on the arm is considered a sign of laziness in the child, and mothers cannot tolerate it. Most mothers want their children to eat quickly, taking big mouthfuls of food. They do not want them to take a long time, eating so slowly that the food is finished by other people before they, the children, are satisfied. This, most women think, tempts children to go back to the cooking pot to steal more food. Again, children are made to keep quiet when they are eating. 'You haven't got two mouths,' they are often told, 'that you can eat with one and talk with the other.'

Toilet training begins very early among the Acholi. When a baby is two to three months old, the mother, in a sitting position, will have him defecate between her legs. From four or five months onwards, or when he is able to sit up alone, he is held in a squatting position by the mother, the nurse, or whoever happens to be near him when he begins to defecate. This system, repeated often enough, gradually becomes the habit of the child. By one-and-a-half years of age, the baby is able to squat by himself. By the time he is two or three years old, and can walk, understand words, and talk, all he usually needs is to be shown where to go when he feels like relieving himself.

Bed-wetting is common and may continue sometimes for four or five years. By then, if the habit is not broken, the child very often suffers scornful words from his parents, relatives and friends. Sometimes he is woken up once or twice in the night to get up and urinate so that he will not wet the bed.

4.

Learning to Get About

The new-born baby is carried very carefully, supported by both hands of the mother or *lapidi*. Or he may be strapped up carefully on to the mother's or nurse's back, or put down on the mother's mat to sleep. The ordinary baby in Acholi has no bed of his own. By three or four months the baby is held in a sitting position supported on the mother's lap, partly because he resents lying flat. He wants to sit up and look at things. When walking or standing, *lapidi* can carry the baby astride her hip. As soon as he can sit up alone, he may be put down on the floor. This practice continues until at about five or six months the baby can sit unsupported; and by six to eight months he will sometimes start crawling. Many babies take much longer than this. Normal children vary widely in their 'motor development'.

At this stage the baby's speed of learning to get about depends in part on the character of the nurse. If the nurse is a very lively active child, she encourages the baby to develop more quickly. An inactive nurse, who spends most of the time sitting quietly with the baby on her lap and does not put him down and play with him, may slow down the speed of his motor development. If the baby can stand up holding on to something or possibly one of the adults, usually the nurse will hold up her hands in a flying position, standing, and say repeatedly and rhythmically, '*Dyedo dyedo a ku-ri*'. (This is difficult to translate. It means something like, 'Come stand, little bird, and try your wings.') In trying to imitate her, the child learns to stand up unsupported. The pleasure achieved by the baby when standing, and the encouragement from the rest of the family, make him learn to stand up firmly. When standing is achieved the nurse holds the baby by both hands and says, '*Tee-te, tee-te*', repeatedly while trying to make him walk. Babies love this, sometimes saying, '*Tee-te*', themselves. These may be the first words they learn to say meaningfully. Sometimes *gara*, or little bells, are tied on to the baby's ankles at this time so that whenever he takes a step, the tiny bells ring. The pleasant sound of these bells encourages the baby to learn to walk more quickly. Some mothers prefer cutting short three-legged sticks which the baby holds on to and pushes when trying to walk.

5.

Sleeping Habits of Acholi Children

During their first year Acholi children are accustomed to being carried on the backs of their mothers or nurses all day. For this reason babies seem to dislike lying down before falling asleep. When a baby is sleepy, he often cries until his mother sits down and gives him the breast. Suckling, he falls asleep, and the mother can lay him down on a bed. Sometimes, to get her baby to sleep, she will tie him on her back as she works and his lack of activity will make him fall asleep.

Although children may go to sleep early in the evening, they will seldom agree to go to bed on their own. Parents threaten them in many ways: 'I will throw you out to a hyena.' 'There is a white man outside.' 'I will shut you out in the darkness.' All these threats make children become so frightened that they will not go to bed on their own. They insist on sitting up with the adults until they finally fall asleep right where they are. Because in most homes of the uneducated villagers, the cooking house is also a bedroom, children cannot be properly put to bed before the adults finish their meal, their drink, their singing, their stories or whatever entertainment they have. Then the mother makes a bed for herself and the children. Sometimes adults sit and eat their supper, *iwang oo*, (round a fire) outside in the courtyard, in which case children lie and sleep out there with them until the adults are ready to go to bed.

A child shares the same mat or room with his parents until he is four or five years old. At this time the child will resent sleeping in his mother's bed, either because he is shunned by his friends for sharing the bed with his parents or because he fears the younger babies will wet him at night. At this time children like sleeping with their older sisters or brothers. The beds of most people in the villages are large papyrus mats. These mats are spread out on the floor, where as many people as can fit on the mat will sleep.

The thirteen-to-sixteen-year-old boy, with the help of his father, builds himself a separate house or 'bachelor hut' to sleep in. Young children are not allowed to play in the boy's house. If he has a sister, it is her responsibility to keep the floor and the walls of the house smartly smeared with black soil. A mother does not ever enter this house. Here a boy collects his friends, sometimes girl friends, and it is taboo for his mother to enter. My brother, aged sixteen, is building his own hut now, with the help of a cousin. They spend all of their school holidays happily planning and building this house, or working his new cotton field.

With the grown up girls it is different. Very often all the girls from the nearby homes, from six years old onwards, collect together and sleep in one house, perhaps with an old woman. It is in this sleeping place that they get their information about sex, since Acholi mothers are sometimes shy, or feel that it is not right to give the young children accurate information about sex. The younger girls in turn are informed by these older ones. It is also in these sleeping groups that girls teach themselves and then practise dancing. Whenever the moon is bright, the girls will dance and play for a long time before going to bed. They work hard at dancing practice in order to compete with the girls of a neighbouring village. Although there may be some very young girls in the group, there are no restrictions about their bed time. Mothers in Acholi are aware that a successful girl must be able to dance well.

Among the educated people this system of sleeping in separate quarters is dying out. Rich educated men now build houses big enough for the whole family to sleep in, the children, as they grow older, leaving their parents' room to join the older children in another room. These days more and more young boys and girls leave home to attend boarding schools, where they spend the larger part of the year.

6.

Traditional Health Practices

When one becomes aware of the conditions under which children in Acholi villages grow up, one is not surprised that such children are often seriously ill. Mothers are careful about washing their babies for the first three months, usually bathing them twice a day. After that the babies are bathed less frequently, perhaps once every day or two until the age of about ten months, after which they will often go several days at a stretch without having a bath. Yet this is the time that children play in the sand and the mud, and tend to smear themselves with all sorts of grime and dirt. Young boys about four years old are often told to join a group of other boys and go to the river or well to wash themselves.

The Acholi people believe, very rightly too, that the health of babies is disturbed when they are teething. What some parents do, even today, some time before the teeth have appeared through the gums, is to take their fretting babies to some local medicine man who will remove the two canine teeth of the lower jaw. Some babies have died as a result of such an operation.

As said before, the Acholi village people want to have as many children as they can. If they have few children they often grow jealous of other parents' children, sometimes, in the case of bad people, going so far as to bewitch or poison the children. It is still very common, when a baby or child is ill, for the mother to suspect that some jealous person is responsible for the disease. That is one of the reasons why some mothers, before they go to the *shamba* or market, say, will be sure to leave some food in the house, telling the children where to find it in their absence. Many mothers, too, will instruct their children not to eat in other people's homes, particularly in the homes of jealous co-wives who, they fear, may try to poison their children.

On the other hand a growing number of Acholi mothers, even village mothers, now take sick babies to hospitals or dispensaries, which are distributed fairly well throughout the district. If modern medical treatment fails, however, or is slow in curing the disease, some mothers will still go to witch doctors or diviners to have them trace the source of the disease.

7.

Growing from Play into Work Activities

After weaning, the child sees less of his mother and more of his nurse, whose job is now to keep him company and to play with him. Very often, the nurse, with the child on her hip or back, will join the company of other nurses and children. Together they form a play group. A large part of the day may be spent by the nurse in this group play while the mother and father of the baby are at work in the home or the field. As said before, when the mother has to be away from the house, she will leave cooked food for the children and tell the nurse where to find it.

Toys are few among Acholi village children. Commercial toys, like dolls, ducks, building bricks, little motor cars, are not given to Acholi children, except in the relatively few homes in which the parents have had a school education and can afford to buy them. Most children are responsible for finding their own play materials. Almost anything can be made into a useful toy by children. Leaves, old tins, maize-cobs, broken pieces of pottery, fruits, seeds, anything they can pick up, will be used by the children as toys. This constant eagerness for toys, on the part of younger children in particular, often leads to the destruction of valuable possessions of the family. Finding at home such fascinating objects as ball-point pens, for example, or even the grown-ups' shoes, young children, having little else to play with and not being allowed to wander about very far, will often put such objects to use in their play. They may afterwards leave them thrown round in the courtyard where parents, upon finding them perhaps in bad condition, may punish the children severely.

Acholi children spend much of their time playing out to their own satisfaction the roles of adults. Little girls can be often observed playing the part of their mothers. They pick up maize-cobs, sticks or bottles, pretending that these are their babies. Sometimes they will sit on the ground, stretching their legs out straight and holding the little 'babies' on their laps. They will take pieces of cloth and tie these make-believe babies on their backs as they see their mothers do. Not long ago I observed one of my sister's children, two and a half years old, carrying her baby. She picked up a tea spoon, and pretended to give some quinine to the doll, 'because the baby is ill', she said. Children of this age, too, particularly the girls, like playing the game of cooking. They will pick up little stones, in place of millet, and start grinding them on the sand. Then, putting together three little stones, they will pretend to make the fire. Old tins and broken pieces of pots are their cooking utensils.

Young boys, already aware of the work of their sex, often like to pull grasses and build little huts. They model motor cars and lorries out of clay. Sometimes they will break off a branch full of leaves, perhaps a big branch, which they use for a motor car. With two or three children astride, they 'drive' rapidly along the ground. Young children want to be active. They like running informal races on their own, climbing trees, singing and dancing. There is no strict grouping of girls and boys in these earlier years. Much of the time they will be seen, and heard, playing together.

A growing number of village children of six to ten now go to primary school. There are still some, however, who do not go, either because their parents cannot afford or do not want to send them to school, or because the nearest school may be four or five miles away, too far for the young child to walk every day. In the latter case, the children may start school when they are older. By this time boys and girls usually stay strictly in their own groups. The separation is encouraged by parents, especially mothers, who feel that it is not proper for their daughters to play among boys. The children themselves have abusive songs which they sing to a child of the opposite sex who may try to join their group. 'Labed, kin litino co!' 'The girl who stays among boys', they will sing, or vice versa. Such songs will usually force the child to leave that company and join the proper one.

For the girls of primary school age their time of playing is nearly over. Home training and stricter discipline begin. At this age the girls must stop eating chicken or any kind of fowl. (An Acholi village woman does not eat any part of a fowl.) The child now has real duties to perform. If she has younger sisters or brothers, she will be a nurse. If she does not have a younger child to look after, and in some cases even if she does, the little girl is expected to make two or three journeys to the well, carrying a small container on her head in which to fetch water. She may be told by her mother who is cooking beans or meat to keep the fire burning. It may be her job also to look after the millet or peas spread out in the sun to dry, keeping the chickens away, collecting and putting the food in the house if it rains. A girl of eight or nine may be expected to grind millet or simsim with her mother, or to accompany her mother into the field to help dig. If her father is away at meal time, the little girl may be asked to take the responsibility of cooking for him, having the food ready by the time he comes back. There is a dual purpose for this thorough training of the girl. It is partly to prepare her for her future duties as a housewife and a mother, and partly to help the mother who, in the Acholi village, has many pressing jobs to do.

The girls who go to school, of course, have much less time for doing any household chores. Many girls have to leave their homes at seven in the morning, returning as late as half-past seven in the evening. From Primary Three, if the school is several miles distant, they cannot come home for lunch. Thus they have little time to practise cooking and other household duties. But some Acholi parents still reserve certain tasks which their primary school girls must perform anyway.

Since most of the secondary schools are boarding schools, the older girls who attend them are away from their homes for the full nine months of the year, and so are out of reach of further traditional training by their mothers. For this reason schools are often considered by Acholi parents to be making their daughters lazy. There is conflict between the school girls and their mothers when they do return home. At school, the girls are taught to be clean and smart, with heavy school assignments but little if any manual work to be done. When they come home they resent having to spend the whole day in the hot sun, weeding in fields with their hands. They dislike having to grind large amounts of millet on the grinding stone. How can they keep clean and smart, they ask, with all these dirty jobs to do? Further, the fact that most of their schools are mixed schools makes many Acholi mothers reluctant to send their daughters to school. They fear that by mixing so much with boys, by learning and speaking English all the time, and by having no practice in traditional manners and housekeeping, the girls are likely to become *malaya* (prostitutes) in the towns. This is one of the reasons why the education of women in Acholi has tended to lag behind.

The boys, on the other hand, are freer from adult attention

until a much later age. From the age of five years, after the separation from the girls, the boys usually play in a gang. They play much wilder games now, too. Shooting or trapping birds is one of their favourite pastimes. They make for themselves *abutidda* or catapults, small Y-shaped twigs of a tree, with rubber strings attached. With these they shoot stones at birds, often going as far as a mile or so from the home to hunt. This takes much of their time. Almost every day, too, they will go in a group to the river to wash their bodies and take a swim.

Another favourite game for Acholi boys at this age is *cobo lawala*. A *lawala* is a willow, bent and tied like a ring about one foot in diameter. Each boy cuts himself a beautiful thin stick about six feet long to use as a spear. The gang divides into two teams. A boy from one team will throw the *lawala* spinning through the air to the other team with all his might, when all of the boys in that team, standing in line, will try to thrust their spears into the centre of the ring. So long as one boy in the team succeeds in spearing and bringing down the *lawala*, the other team will keep throwing it for them to spear. A boy who is an expert at *lawala* is always very good at hunting, too. He will seldom miss the running animal when he goes hunting. Because boys who go to school do not have the time required for practising *lawala*, they can never hope to be really good hunters with spears. As more and more Acholi boys now go to school, the game of *lawala* is gradually dying out.

8.

The Acholi Parents as Teachers

Children's relationships with their parents depend, first of all, on the age of the children. Young babies are very close to their mothers or nurses. Most fathers in Acholi do not have a close relationship with babies. It is a woman's job to look after them, as said earlier. Moreover, Acholi men spend most of the day away from their homes. After digging in the morning, they eat their meal, then go off to visit their friends or attend beer parties.

After weaning, even the mother-child relationship breaks considerably. The child now spends most of his time with the nurse. If the mother has no nurse, she may take her child to join some other group of children, where she will leave him to play until she returns. This happens when the child has become too heavy to be carried about, or the mother has another baby to take his place. Sometimes such children are taken to their grand-mothers' to be looked after. There is a tendency, however, for grandparents to 'spoil' children by over-feeding and perhaps carrying them on their backs even if they are too heavy. For this reason, mothers hesitate to send their children to stay for long periods with their grandparents.

Child-parent relationships also depend on the sex of the child. After weaning, boys do not have a close relationship with their mothers any more. From two to six years old, a boy spends most of his time with a nurse, and then with a gang of other boys. When a boy is about eight years old, he can accompany his father to the garden to dig, although very often he is excused to come home earlier than his father. His mother will give him food and, after eating, off he goes to play. In the early evenings he may go with his father for a walk round the fields or into the jungle to collect some logs. These logs are burned in the courtyard fire which the family gathers to sit around in the evening. The boy is usually told to sweep the compound before he lights the evening fire.

When he grows a little older, the father will show him the total area of his field, where it starts and where it ends, so that in future nobody can take it from him. During their walks in the evening, father and son carry spears. A father will tell his son to carry a spear or two whenever he goes to the jungle, in case an animal or an enemy appears. He tells the young boy all he knows about the behaviour of certain dangerous animals, and what to do when they appear. He shows him which trees are good, or bad, for building houses or grain stores, for making a hoe, and so on. Gradually, as the boy grows older, he is able to fetch the logs and make the fire without being told or helped.

The expansion of school education, and especially of boarding schools, has seriously weakened this father-son relationship. Day school boys do come home in the evening, when they are expected to sweep the compound and light the evening fire. In the evening the boy sits outside by the fire with his father while the mother is still preparing supper.

The girls, on the other hand, spend more time with their mothers from the beginning. Almost as soon as the girl passes the breast-feeding stage, she is given little jobs to do. She goes to the garden with her mother, perhaps helping or pretending to help with a very small hoe. She also goes with her mother to fetch firewood. Acholi mothers pay great attention to the development of their little daughters. If even the young child shows a tendency towards being lazy in doing these small home duties, the mother may become very worried about her. She may even beat the girl for it. (I remember my own mother slapping me on the face because at ten years of age I had not learned to grind millet well.) In the late evening, when father and brother are sitting out by the fire, the little girl stays inside, helping her mother get the food ready. Again, girls who go to school have less time with their mothers. They are therefore considered lazy and inefficient house-workers by traditional Acholi standards.

Child-parent relationships depend, thirdly, on whether or not the father has other wives. A man with many wives may decide to build all the wives' houses together around one compound or, to avoid too much quarrelling between the co-wives, he can scatter their homes over fairly great distances. In the latter case all of the children tend to have too little attention from their fathers. The young boy has to go and dig with his mother in her small garden instead of accompanying his father. Boys in such homes, because they hardly know their father except when he punishes them, often dislike their father, and tend to build up fear and ill feeling towards him. When quarrels or fights occur between the parents, the children will usually side with the mother against the father.

Children whose mothers are dead or divorced and some children of *luk* or unmarried women, are usually taken, sometimes unwillingly, into the houses of stepmothers. If the stepmother dislikes them, the children may have very harsh treatment, and perhaps be underfed. Surprisingly enough, some girls brought up in this way become very efficient housewives by Acholi standards. By making them work too hard, the stepmothers often train them to be very tough and strong.

As I have said before, it is the concern of all the relatives, not only the parents, to bring up the child properly and make him fit into and be useful in the village community. It is, therefore, a duty of the growing child to obey all his relatives. He is strictly taught by his parents to say nothing rude to anybody, including relatives. A little girl can be asked by any woman in the village to grind some millet, fetch some water, or cook something for her. Any male relative can request a little boy to run an errand, or help him in some other way. Children are expected to do all of these things without complaining. Those who do not obey will always have a bad reputation in the village. They are often told the proverb, *Lalek camo wi ogwang mutwo.* 'The child who cannot do any favour for people, eats the bony skull of a wild cat.' Or the other proverb, *Okwero pwony cito ki cet pa maro.* 'If you do not listen to people's advice, you will go mannerless to your mother-in-law's home.' This would be a disgrace, of course. The place where every man or every woman should show the best behaviour is in a mother-in-law's house.

9.

Discipline in Tribal Education

There is a constant attempt on the part of the adults, then, to mould the character and behaviour of children. A child who talks too much or asks too many questions is discouraged by the adults from so doing. A child who cries often without a real cause is whipped by the father, mother, or a relative until he keeps quiet.

The girls from the earliest years tend to be more disciplined and restricted than the boys. In the ordinary village home in Acholi, children often go about naked. For this reason mothers are very particular about the way in which little girls sit. From one and a half years onwards, the girl is repeatedly told and warned to sit down smartly with her knees together. If even a small girl sits carelessly, she may be whipped by the mother. I have twin nieces, aged two and a half, who already are so particular about their sitting habits that they keep reminding each other to sit properly. They often tell the adults to see how well they sit.

Another strict rule for the girls is that they should keep close to the homestead. No mother wants her four to six-year-old daughter wandering from home to home. This is considered a very bad and dangerous practice, which may lead to poisoning, as already said, or to future prostitution of the girl. Nevertheless a group of girls are permitted to go together to the well or out to fetch firewood.

Girls also have to obey their big brothers, who have authority over their younger siblings. A fifteen-year-old boy may order his sister to cook quickly for him because he is in a hurry to go to a dance. He may order her to clean his house or to fetch him some water for washing his clothes. The girl must respond to these orders in perfect obedience. Failure to do so often leads to a fight between the two children, almost always to the disadvantage of the girl, who may be the smaller or physically weaker of the two. Parents tend to ignore or even encourage these incidents, since the role of the Acholi female is to be obedient. 'You will suffer great blows from somebody's son if you do not practise obedience now,' the girls are often told.

Older brothers are also very particular about the way their

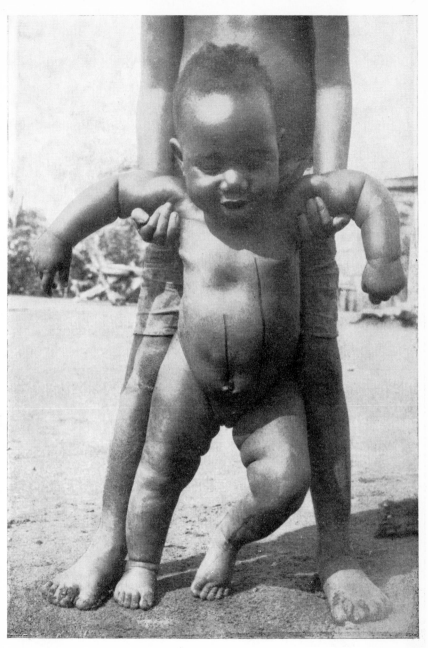

'. . . . . I would hold her arms and, with a tune "Teee teee teee," make her feet
move one after the other.'

Then, as now, before the baby was a year old, her breast feeding would be 'supplemented with solid food'.

The girls 'would have with them containers in which to draw water, thereby helping the mothers . . . . .'

The duty of 'collecting and carrying firewood was felt essentially to be girls' work'.

'We would make use of such simple materials as sand, soil . . . . .' for modelling and for play.

'Whoever hit the target (a bush, a tree, a rock, a bird) at first attempt, would be exempt
from some of the (herding duties).'

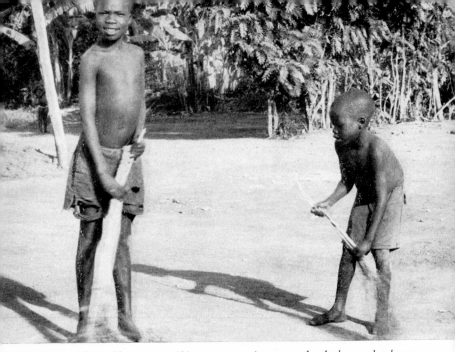

Boys with no older sister would have to sweep the compound and take on other home duties 'usually performed by the girls'.

Today 'the child enters school very early in life . . . (so that almost before he has had time to learn much of his own culture) the intensive process of Europeanization begins'.

'Radios these days, transistor or otherwise.......are in a growing number of homes.'

'Travel for many youngsters is done on bicycles', either their own or those borrowed from father or brother.

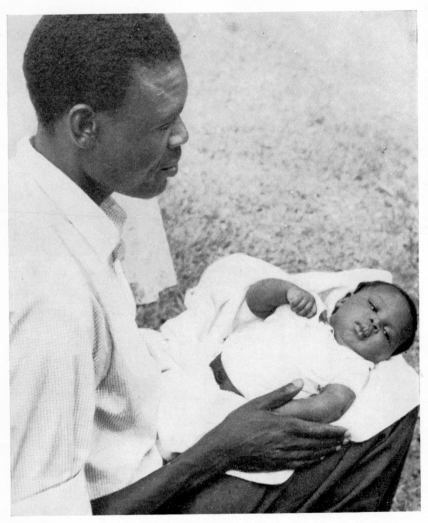

'Fathers now take a keener interest in children, especially babies, than ever before.'

Increasingly, both new and expectant mothers 'make frequent visits to the clinic and consult other experts'.

'. . . lapidi (the nurse) is the second mother to the baby, and there are some babies who are fonder of their lapidi than of their own mothers.'

'*A mother who does not have lapidi is bound to carry her baby about wherever she goes and whatever she does.*'

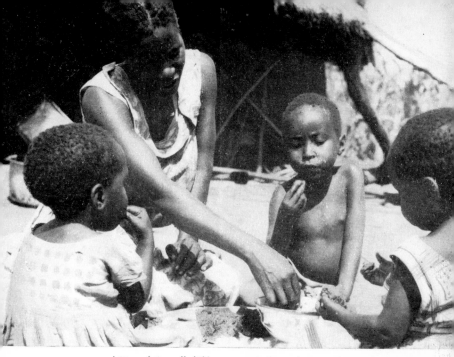

'At meal time all children eat with the mother . . . . .'

They *'like to pull grasses and build little huts . . . . . There is no strict grouping of girls and boys in these earlier years'.*

Girls who attend the secondary boarding schools 'are out of reach of further traditional training by their mothers'.

'The thirteen-to-sixteen-year-old boy, with the help of his father, builds himself a separate house or "bachelor hut" to sleep in.'

'By this time (from the age of fifteen onwards) an Acholi girl is highly accomplished by traditional standards.'

'Often it seems to be only the oldest villagers who ponder and treasure the past.'

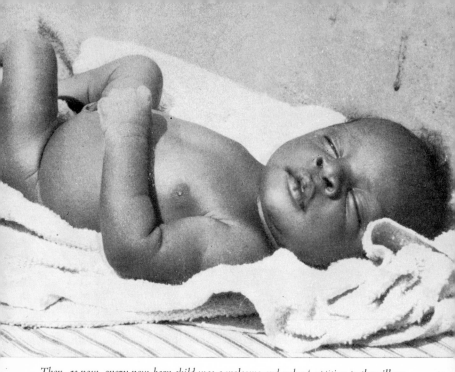

Ther, as now, every new-born child was a welcome and valued addition to the village.

Small boys would play at building their houses in the fields not too far from home.

How often a first-born son has had to give up play with his friends to look after a younger child!

Herding was after all a pleasant task for the Kamba boy, who always knew that before long he would be joined by his playmates.

grown up sisters behave in the presence of their boy friends If a boy sees his sister misbehaving in any way, he is authorized by his parents to give her a good beating. The sisters are very important to the brothers, whose future can largely depend on them. A brother whose sister has good manners and is married is sure to have a wife himself. The money paid to his father as his sister's bride price is the money he will use for his own marriage. Since he cannot marry until his sister is married, it is his real concern to see that she is well-behaved enough to be married early.

Acholi parents do not like their children to steal things. If even a young child shows a tendency towards stealing, he is severely punished by beating; he may be denied his meals for a whole day, or until he confesses and promises to steal no more.

10.

The Adolescent Years

From the age of fifteen years onwards, children are treated in a much more respectful manner. Everybody in the village accepts the fact that the child *odoko dano*, has become a person. No mother wants to beat her daughter at this age. It would be considered a shameful disgrace. If the girl does anything wrong the mother corrects her in words only. Or, she may refer her to an aunt or some older relative who will give her advice.

By this time an Acholi village girl is highly accomplished by traditional standards. She does most of the cooking in the home now, doing everything without being told. She knows, or ought to know, exactly what her duties are. A mother with a grown-up girl is very lucky. For almost the first time, in many cases, the Acholi mother can go and relax with her friends, knowing that the daughter is performing the household duties well in her absence. When the mother is at home, she can sit and instruct the girl as she works. No good girl can sit and do nothing while the mother is working. This would give her a bad reputation, which could make her marriage difficult. There are many songs composed to warn such girls.

> *Min anyaka too ka rego*
> *Colo nyaka pe*
> *Nyako obedo kilao*
> *Min anyaka too yo kulu*
> *Calo nyaka pet*
> *Nyako obedo kilao.*

> The mother of the girl
> Suffers all the way
> Going to the well
> Grinding and so on
> As if she has no daughter to help her.
> This girl is hopeless.

The Acholi girls at this stage, educated or not, are usually very particular about cleanliness, of their bodies and of the house. On entering any home in the village one can tell, from the appearance of the house, whether there is an adolescent girl in the family. A house where there is such a girl is usually kept constantly and smartly smeared with black soil. Along the wall, the girl will hang rows of clean white calabashes, very cleverly decorated. Some have *adungu*, a musical instrument played by girls, hanging up there, too. Outside, somewhere behind the house, one sees a heap of firewood neatly tied up into bundles. These are the signs of the presence of a wonderful girl in the home. Such a girl is likely to have a lot of suitors coming and going.

The adolescent boy is treated respectifully, too. The presence of an adolescent boy, or boys, in the home is indicated by an extra house or houses, in the compound, the bachelor huts. Each grown up boy is entitled to a hut of his own. He is highly respected by his mother, who keeps a separate dish for him whenever she cooks. Each year, the boy must, by himself or with the help of his father, open an acre of cotton for his own use. My brother, who is sixteen has got the first acre of cotton to which he is entitled.

Boys of this age spend a lot of their time away from the home. Nobody minds where they go nor at what time of night they come back to their huts. At this age it is considered normal and proper for a boy to go out looking for a wife. Any father would be worried, and suspect that something was wrong with his son, if he did not show these signs. In case of any misconduct by the boy—for example, if he gets a girl into trouble—the father always pays the necessary fine for it, and does so without much complaint. The mother, contrary to what one would suppose, tends to be happy when her son does this. She expects, and it does happen, that the girl who is in trouble will soon come and spend a few months with her until the illegal baby is delivered. During her stay with the boy's family, she will relieve his mother of her household duties. This is a time of trial for the girl, however. Just like a student teacher on teaching practice, she must show her talents if she hopes to get married into the family, and the whole society approves of this. The result is that such girls tend to be over-worked in the boy's, or what turns out to be the mother-in-law's, home.

11.

Postscript

In Acholi today there are hundreds of families who live exactly as I have explained above. This includes most of the people in my own clan, although changes are beginning to affect them also. Our old clan forest, beginning several miles outside of Gulu, extends for some twenty-eight miles. Many family farms are included in this stretch, a few of them very progressive. My father's farm is one of these. We raise cotton, millet, maize, simsim, cassava, groundnuts and all our own fruits and garden vegetables. My four sisters and I, my brother, my late mother, my present stepmother, my father and some of his brothers, all worked in the fields when I was growing up. We still love farm life. My sister, who has just returned from almost two years of Infant Teacher Training in England, tells us how she used to miss the work in the fields, especially during the long vacations. Her British friends could hardly believe that this was true. I myself, when I was home for the recent Easter break from Makerere College, sowed our entire groundnut crop, and was proud to do it. Now several months later, the groundnuts have matured and are ready to be harvested. My sister, my cousins, or my father perhaps, will pull the groundnut plants in my absence, leaving them in the field to dry in the sun. We can do this because, as my sister remarked, the population of our area are still good people. There is no stealing yet. It is sad to think that only as civilization comes to Acholi communities are the people beginning to steal, so that farmers soon will not be able to leave their groundnuts or maize or other crops safely in the fields to dry.

For this is a period of rapid development in East Africa. The old economic and social structure is disintegrating in many ways. Gradually it is being replaced by a money economy. There are Acholi fathers who go from the village now to earn money in the towns. Some of these men leave their wives in the village, there to produce the food for their families, while the men work for money in the towns. When they have earned what they feel is enough, these fathers come back to the village. Some of the younger men who, having received some Primary or Junior Secondary education, find work in the towns, may take their wives and young children with them. They are able to buy more or less permanent homes on the outskirts, or rent houses provided in quarters or housing estates inside the towns. This class of men is increasing rapidly in Acholi. Most of them work as clerks, office messengers, and such. They are joined by the growing number of teachers, better educated, who also leave their homes or villages to teach in whatever schools they are assigned to. In this class of people, the men or women will earn money and that is all. Their farming or food production is limited to small vegetable gardens. Most of the family food is bought at the market.

Other changes in the practices I have described are gradually, sometimes rapidly, taking place in Acholi villages. These days, for example, more and more children are born in maternity centres or hospitals where none of the old tribal traditions are kept. The placenta and the umbilical cords of babies born in hospitals, instead of being buried in certain places to insure their good health in the future, are destroyed at once. It is nurses now, instead of mothers or mothers-in-law, who look after the women in labour. This is a choice that a gradually growing number of Acholi village women are making, realizing that maternity centres and hospitals offer more security against the many dangers traditionally involved in childbirth. In the centres too, the mothers are given instructions on better ways to look after their babies.

This means also that the special ceremonies for pregnant women are slowly dying out. But one thing still exists, strongly. A young married woman is expected to become pregnant within the first few months of her marriage. If she does not, she will begin to get scornful words or ill treatment from the relatives of her husband.

A few other changes affecting the care of Acholi children should be mentioned. Take eating practices. The custom by which several families have their meals together is restricted to villages now where it is still quite common, especially among the uneducated or less-educated families. Village families which go to the towns will usually eat their own food. It is still common practice, however, even in the towns, for the children to be given their meals separately. Many town wives eat separately too, their working men unable to come home for food in the middle of the day. The men are often too late in returning home in the evenings also for their wives and the children to wait.

There are some Acholi families, especially the families of teachers, where husband and wife eat together at a table.

Sleeping facilities for children are improving. In most educated Acholi homes now, babies and other children have beds of their own. Most working men living in towns have proper beds for their children as well as for themselves. In a few very advanced homes, the mothers have prams in which their babies can be pushed and can sleep. It is usually only when these families come back to visit their village relatives that the mats are again spread out on the floor for their sleeping.

Many of these improvements are coming about because of the changing attitudes of Acholi villagers towards school education. The Uganda Ministry of Education figures for June 1965 indicate that eighty per cent of the school-age children in Acholi attend Government schools. Even in the villages, the number is growing rapidly. This has been a tremendous development, bringing improvements in many aspects of living. In the primary school, for example, all children are given health training. They are taught to wash their bodies every day, to keep their nails and hair short, to brush their teeth. And to make sure that they do all of this, some teachers require the children to do it in school every day. This is bound to have a good effect on the school-age children. Already there is a striking difference in the young village child who goes to school and the one who does not. Recently my young cousin, a first-born about to start primary school, said to his mother, 'From next month onwards, you are going to have trouble. Who do you think then will have the awful job of caring for your crying baby?'

The changing attitudes of Acholi villagers towards the school education of girls is especially important. So often I think how well my elder sisters would have done in life if they had been given opportunities for education similar to mine. In their childhood, though, as I have said earlier, it was almost unthinkable for girls to be sent to school. I remember that even in my junior secondary school days, a group of us were taken with a travelling show into villages for fifty miles round, to try to teach the villagers the value of sending their daughters to school. By now many Acholi parents have seen that educated girls can become nurses, teachers or secretaries, and can earn a good livelihood. An increasing number then are sending both sons and daughters to school, with the hard-working mothers especially making sacrifices to pay the school fees. It is most likely that in a few years the Acholi will have many women going on to the University Colleges. I have the honour of being the first. Two others will be joining me at Makerere in the near future.

So it is that with the growing cash economy, the trend towards the towns, and the spread of school education for both men and women, the horizons of Acholi children and young people, even in the villages, are gradually growing wider. Improved transportation facilities are used by more and more people. Better roads are being built all over Uganda, some of them in Acholi going from village to village. Many families in once remote village homes have their night's sleep interrupted, until they become accustomed to the sound, by the constant line of huge lorries that go grinding up and down the slopes at night taking produce to market. The whistle and rumble of trains breaks the silence in many places, since two years ago the railway line was extended across Acholi. From time to time an aeroplane will fly high over Acholi towns and villages. Then even the very young children may look up and, pointing to the moving object, merely remark, 'Aeroplane, Mummy!' Swift and comfortable buses cover the distance between Acholi towns and Kampala in a matter of hours, a journey which in my own childhood took days.

The first time I travelled by bus, I remember, was in 1948, when I was seven years old. I cannot forget that first ride. I was travelling with my mother to my grandmother's house, about thirty-five miles away. I can still hear the noise of the engine and feel the bumping of the bus. It all seemed strange and frightening to me then, especially when I made a remarkable discovery. Wondering if we would ever get to Grandmother's house, I turned round to look at the passengers behind me. They were not moving at all. Everyone in the bus was sitting still, remaining in exactly the same position. When I looked out of the window I saw that it was the trees and the grass and the houses along the road that were moving, not the people on the bus! To me this was an amazing sight. I was still wondering and trying to figure it all out, when the bus stopped. 'Come out, Apoko, come out!' my mother was saying. For we had reached my grandmother's home.

Again, some Acholi children come from rich families who, instead of using bicycles, can own their own cars, thus making it possible for the families to do much more travelling. Motor cars from the towns and cities go whizzing by on the main roads, past the schools and homes and market places where children can always be found. Along these same roads, still, there will always be a constant stream of people walking, especially on market days. Men and boys can be seen with their bicycles, frequently carrying a friend or a wife or child, and sometimes both, or a heavy load of produce up hill and down. The women will be carrying headloads of firewood, perhaps, containers of water, or large loads of market produce. Often they will have babies tied on their backs, with sometimes another child or two clinging to their skirts as the cars flash by. For the Acholi village men, except for the few like my father who truly like to do farm work, are still prone to follow more leisurely pastimes— hunting, chatting in the market, attending funerals, drinking beer—leaving their women to carry the brunt of the heavy work. My Acholi classmate, a man, always argues with me about this. But I have observed much too much of the respective responsi- bilities carried by the men and boys and the women and girls in my tribe, even nowadays, to feel that I can agree with him. Many times on market days, one will see adolescent girls carrying their headloads along the road, quite obviously annoyed by boys of about their own age who may follow or taunt them. The market place is still a popular place for Acholi adolescents to make friends of the opposite sex.

Children and young people, at school and sometimes at home, are having more access to radio. The primary child who can still tell an old Acholi folk tale in dramatic detail, singing the songs in the story with gusto, also knows how to sing and twist to some of the current 'pop songs'. Dr. Obote is the Presi- dent of Uganda, of course. And even the youngest child, where there is a radio in the home, will want to twist to this song, *Ye yekka Obote waffe*, or 'He alone, our Obote.' Children also pick up stories from the radio, for Radio Uganda broadcasts children's programmes in most Uganda languages now. The older children, along with their parents, often listen to the news. Thus with the increasing number of radio and even, as time goes on, television sets accessible to Acholi families and schools, it is likely that our children in the future will have better facilities for learning. Already they are becoming increasingly accustomed to modern changes and improvements. More and more of them are learning many of the old tribal customs by word of mouth from their elders, not through experience as we did. Often it seems to be only the oldest villagers who ponder and treasure the past. The children and youth are more apt to enjoy the modern and look to the future.

THORNS IN THE GRASS:

The Story of a Kamba Boy

by

J. Mutuku Nzioki

1.

Not Meant for Young Ears

Our rectangular house was two-roomed, built of unburnt bricks and grass-thatched. The inside was plastered with white clay. Our kitchen was circular and some ten yards away from the house. It was made of the same material as the sleeping house but was not plastered. On the whole, when compared to the five or six other homes in the village, ours ranked among the best.

The village was small, the people poor, the richest villager having but a few head of cattle. No one had a really big field for grazing. All the cattle and goats from the village grazed together in some isolated grazing grounds. One villager was a teacher, and great was the respect he got from all the villagers, the young and the old alike. We children would always run to take his message somewhere, or stand up when he passed by and, however much the worse for drink, threatened to take us to school. This we did not want. We had always heard from the older boys that if anyone went to school his buttocks would pain all day long from 'the sticks'.

It did not seem that any one in the village took its great

poverty into account. They were all satisfied with what they had. The oldest man in the village appeared most contented. When he was not drunk, he would be found either lying in the shade of a tree near his hut or, if it was the season, cultivating his small *shamba*. Whenever he came home drunk towards sunset, we would all enjoy the song he would sing to herald his own arrival:

> Beautiful girl, you will be married.
> Do not cry because of marriage.
> Good company will come to an end.
> Oh beautiful girl, you will be married.
> Do not cry because of marriage.
> Even if you cry, you will have to get married;
> Beautiful girl, you will be married.
> You will bring wealth to your father.

We had learned it after many days of listening and would join in as he sang—at a safe distance in case he would think we were mocking him and strike us with his long stick. With the song he was really praising his last daughter, who was at that time the only mature unmarried girl in our small village. We knew she was then being hunted by men. Many were the unknown gentlemen who stooped to conquer us by making temporary friendship, as we played on the road that ran near the village.

'You all say we are friends,' one of these would say to us. This was fine and friendly.

'Yes, we are friends,' a brave boy would answer on our behalf.

'Then whom shall we send to call the girl from that home for us?' another would ask.

'Me,' from the boldest of us.

'It is good. You are a real male!'

Then we would run and tell the old man's daughter that some people were calling her.

At first she would refuse or pretend that she did not hear, particularly when her mother was present. After a short time, though, she would pick up a rope and say she was going to fetch firewood, or maybe take a gourd and decide to go to draw water. We would all follow her and when we reached the men, she would request us to go back. At times we would refuse, thinking it was great fun to tease her. We might hang around until one of the men would threaten to break up our friendship if we did not disappear. We would then run away, singing the song her father adored so much.

Then we would say, '*Po, Um, Cho!*' and spit on the ground in the way the old man did. 'I am not poor by any means,' we would continue, imitating him. 'I have two hands with which I can find wealth. I hear you call me poor, you dogs, may you die without cause like skinny dogs. *Po, Um, Cho!*' and we would spit continuously.

The village old man was not the only one to be heard making the declaration that he was 'not poor'. I cannot say the number of drunkards who loudly claimed to be not poor, as they passed along the road. Surprisingly, I cannot recall having heard any one declare that he was rich. Indeed, some would pass by at night shouting loudly and proudly, that all the villagers were poor, and poor they would all die.

'What is that drunkard talking about? Who has done him wrong? Does he not know that wealth is provided by God?' my mother would complain.

One afternoon, as we sat inside on stools beside a pot in which food was boiling for supper, a soft *Hodi* came from the door. Perhaps the noise made by the pot-cover tossing up and down drowned the woman's voice for my mother. I felt like saying, 'Come in!' But I knew that was my mother's job. The woman outside said *Hodi* once more and my mother called 'Come in!' The woman entered and asked if she had not heard her say '*Hodi*'.

'I have been saying *Hodi* for seasons,' she muttered.

'Forgive us, we were not hearing. You see the pot is making a lot of noise,' apologized my mother. Then to me she said:

'Uo, will you not give this woman the stool you are sitting on?' I surrendered the stool instantly.

'Why are you staying with your mother like a girl,' the woman asked me as she took the stool, 'while the other boys are playing outside?'

Without giving answer, I rushed out, disappearing into the village. Another boy joined and chased me for some distance. He was Paulo, my paternal cousin and closest playmate. The previous evening we had been playing a game of 'Touch and Pass Bad Omen,' whereby the person to be touched last bears all the bad omen in the world. Since I had touched this boy last, it was no wonder he chased me as soon as he saw me, in an attempt to pass the bad omen back.

It was drizzling a little, so I headed for the nearest house. Knowing full well that if I stopped at the door to call *Hodi!*

Paulo would touch me, I dashed right in. He followed and we stood inside, panting and wiping our faces, but for a moment only.

'Out, you skinny dogs!' ordered my aunt. We had entered her house the improper way and this annoyed her. She had a visitor, a pregnant woman from outside our village. The two women appeared to be having a private chat.

We retreated at once and I sped away. Paulo gave chase but after a few yards the raindrops hit us harder. We ran back to find shelter along the verandah of my aunt's hut.

'Please don't pass Bad Omen to me now,' I said to Paulo. 'You see it is raining and we cannot chase each other. If you do so, it will be a fight. Do you understand that?' Paulo was smaller than I, and feared me. He smiled away my warning and did not come near me.

Sitting on the verandah, we overheard from my aunt's hut the following conversation, obviously not meant for young ears.

'As I left off telling you when those silly boys came in . . . When I was pregnant last, he never bought any sugar for me to take tea when I delivered. I don't really know what he thinks of me. He does not understand that I am carrying his child in my womb.'

'And why I don't know,' my aunt said. 'Men seem to value babies as soon as the babies can say, "I am yours, father," and not until then. But do not trouble yourself. God can help your child so he will place you in such luxury as you have never dreamed of.'

Then the talk was directed towards a village girl who had become pregnant accidentally. The two women agreed that the girl was not only stupid, unfortunate, of ill fate, but that she had got her just reward. The visitor repeated that pregnancy had served the village girl right, but withdrew her statement as soon as she had made it.

'Let me not say this. After all my daughter may be pregnant tomorrow,' she said.

'Why do unmarried girls get fireplace pregnancy? Cannot they bear and overcome the temptation? Anyway let me not say this loudly for there may be some ears beyond the wall,' and my aunt toned her voice low.

'Do you know what fireplace pregnancy is, if you are all that clever?' Paulo asked me softly.

'Yes, it is the pregnancy of a girl who is not married,' I answered.

'Uum. So you know. Anyway you are right.'

The drizzle was not so bad now, so we sneaked away, lest our steps betray us to the women inside.

'Then it is now or never,' Paulo declared suddenly.

I understood what he meant and adopted swift long strides to avoid his touching me. He gave chase and this time we ended inside my grandmother's mud hut.

The thatch of the hut was pitch black with soot that had accumulated over the years. The inside was smoky from burning wet Eucalyptus leaves, making our eyes shed tears, the usual introduction into the ever-smoking hut. The old woman was accustomed to it. When anyone complained, she would rebuke him and say that she did not want that type of showing-off inside her house.

Granny had not yet noticed our presence. She had been too busy blowing at the fire. Beside her sat a village woman, the wife of my father's half-brother, whose belly for months had been swollen with child. That day she seemed to have her shoulders bent forward and she looked sickish. I thought she might give birth that very hour. The previous night, I had heard the same woman telling my mother that she was sick. When Granny turned round to face us, we started to retreat. We all feared her nails, knowing how much pain they could cause to our thighs if we had wronged her and she managed to get hold of us.

'So you think your grandmother's hut is yours to pop into, running, any time of the day? Paulo, come and blow this fire for me,' Granny said, failing to pronounce 'p' and substituting 'm' instead.

The boy blew the fire and set it in flames that further menaced the sooty roof, then withdrew quickly. We never trusted Granny, even after rendering her some valuable service. She could change instantly, grabbing hold of one of us and plunging her nails into his thighs, with commands never to misbehave again. She was good at imparting discipline, was Granny.

'When is your husband going to come?' Granny asked the pregnant mother.

'I don't know. He sent a letter the other day and said he would come today. But where is he? Don't you know that men are not pleased with pregnant wives?'

It was already sunset, and I thought I would trick Paulo as I did not want him to touch me and pass Bad Omen. So I said to him, 'Paulo, go and draw water for me. I am very thirsty.'

'Where is the water mug?' Paulo asked Granny.

'What for?' retorted the old woman.

'For water. Eaa! And what is the matter?' asked Paulo.

'Um, the water you drew for me last year, or which?' queried Granny.

'I don't want to joke with you, please. Tell me where the water mug is,' requested Paulo.

'Take it from behind the pot. And inform your friend that you will go and draw water for me tomorrow. Do you understand that?'

As Paulo approached the water pot, I ran out laughing, leaving him behind, with Granny saying, 'I knew your friend did not want water. He wanted to leave you and here you are. The small friend is gone. He has run out. Follow!'

As for me, I ran straight into my mother's kitchen. She was seated near the fireplace, where my small sister of four years or so was sitting beside her, on the ground. On her little thighs was sitting a baby, my brother. My sister tried hard to maintain her balance with the little fellow. No one had forced her to hold my brother. She claimed the right to 'nurse' the baby herself, and was allowed to do so, in spite of the fact that she was so very small. Once she did sway and was just about to topple over when my mother helped. I laughed. It was very amusing to see the little woman fail in what she thought she was so capable of doing. From the pot came the appealing smell of green maize and beans and I knew supper would be ready soon.

I was served supper in a small white bowl which was mine for every meal. I was the first-born and no doubt the pride of my mother. She was much concerned about my meals and always insisted that I should take much. After supper, she would tell me a story, as usual. This night, she told of a small young orphan, probably of my own age. He had travelled far, with roasted sweet potatoes for meals but no water. At last the orphan came to a dry plain with tufts of grass here and there. He was just dying of thirst. Water was nowhere to be found. The boy sat near a tuft and sang:

> Tuft be uprooted, tuft be uprooted,
> Who will draw for me? Tuft be uprooted

Tuft be uprooted for the thirsty child
My father's wife gives me under-cooked food
And I eat and sleep;
Tuft be uprooted for the thirsty child.

Then the tuft would jump into the air and water would spring up for the thirsty boy to drink. This made me sleepy in no time as had many other stories. I still tried to listen in spite of the fact that I was dozing, supported by my mother's hands lest I plunge my face into the smouldering fire. Finally we went to bed.

Sleep defeated me very quickly on this particular night, though not my mother. I had been sleeping for a period, I don't know how long, when I suddenly woke up feeling the coldness of my wet blanket. At some seasons I proved to be a real bed-wetter. 'Tuft, be uprooted for the thirsty child,' I found myself still mumbling as I awoke. When I uncovered my head, Kale, my father's half-brother and husband of the pregnant village woman we had seen at Granny's, was there standing at the foot of my bed near the door. My mother was busy at an old cupboard looking for something unknown to me.

'Take a razor blade and some sewing thread if you can obtain any. And for heaven's sake, hurry up!' the man was saying. 'The other women are waiting for you.'

In a jiffy my mother was gone. What was the matter? Of course, I remembered, the woman had given birth. This I knew when Kale, upon noticing the wet patch on the bed, had inquired if I was getting a third sibling while I was still a bed-wetter. He was ignorant, so I felt. I wondered if he ever understood that bed-wetting was done while one was not aware of it. He ordered me to move to the farthest end of the bed. This I had already done to avoid the wet portion.

I was probably the only kid in the village lucky enough to possess such a bed. It was a big one. The framework was wooden, with sisal ropes woven into a net to join the framework. It was covered with two old sacks and a few rags for bedding. There was no mattress and, anyway, I think none would have lasted a week with that nightly spring from me. Kale felt the wet portion of the bed and covered it with some rags. Then he lay down beside me.

You can expect rags that have been soaked with urine nearly every night to be smelly. They had a repelling stench, which I could hear Kale breathe in and sneeze out. The smell was no problem to me. I was used to it and could cover myself fully, falling asleep with ease.

'Now small boy, listen to me and I will tell you. If you wet the bed again, I will pinch your thighs so hard that they will bleed. Do you hear?'

'Yes,' I said, and felt fear grip me. Then we slept.

The next morning Kale woke me very early. When my mother came in, I could see that the sun was shining outside. I loved basking in the morning sun. So, jumping out of bed, I slipped into my pants and shirt and prepared to march out. I would first go and warm myself from that heavenly body, until my mother would call and order me to wash my face before breakfast. But this morning, I did not bask in such ease. My mother gave me a job as she left, heading for the hut of Kale.

'When the baby wakes up and cries, come and call me. Do you hear that, you child? Leave him to fall down and then you will tell me what you were doing when I come back. Bask, but listen at the same time.'

'And where are you going, leaving the child with me?' I complained.

'I am going to that hut. Do you mean to say you don't know that we got another baby last night?' And with that she disappeared round the house.

Kale had had cause to come and disturb me in my own bed after all. By Kamba custom he could not occupy the same house as the woman who had given birth. Besides, his presence during delivery would have been eyed with great contempt by the women.

Too much noise now came from the direction of the hut where birth had occurred. Who was there making the noise? Who but the village women and their daughters? The girls fitted well into their mothers' company. The boys were ordered out when, now and then, they tried to peep in to see what important operations were taking place.

When the baby cried, whose cry I had been ordered to listen for, I dashed to take the message to my mother. The house of Kale was very near and I was at the door in no time.

'Excuse me. If you see him here, it means the baby is awake now,' my mother said as she took leave. I lingered around the door for some time before I was ordered away by an old woman not really from our village. But not before I had seen a good deal.

The women were taking tea from mugs, and some of the big girls from small containers made from gourds. The number was too large for them all to be served tea in mugs at one time. Any one could tell from the outside that something outstanding had occurred under the roof of that hut. I had never heard the village women talk so loudly, so happily and, above all in such a co-operative manner. They were all friends alike as they celebrated the arrival of a child. One villager, however, did not stay long to share in the chat. The village's witch, probably fearing that anything wrong that happened would surely be attributed to her, slipped away without notice.

We boys were served tea after the women and the girls had had their fill. When I went back to our house, I asked my mother why she had taken a razor blade and thread.

'Are you a small fool?', she asked.

'Why?'

'Au, I was telling you that the razor blade was used to cut the umbilical cord of the child. It was cut just as yours was,' she said, touching the remains of mine.

The news of the birth of the baby must have spread like wild fire. Friends, relatives and neighbours came one after the other, all women, talking and talking by way of celebration. Men did not seem to take it as a great occasion. The village men did not in any way show that they felt joy at the clean delivery. Perhaps they talked about it when they went to drink beer somewhere. But weeks and even months later, some of the women present, and still others who had not been there the day following the birth, would come bringing gifts to the baby. These included bananas, pieces of sugar cane, bread, and other nice things.

'We have come to hold the baby,' one of them would say.

This they would do and then give to the mother several coins, usually ten-cent pieces or even shillings, but never notes, in payment for the privilege of holding her child.

We liked these women visitors very much. The bananas and the sugar cane they brought meant much to us. We were never refused a share. I felt that even if we were not entertained at the birth of the child, we definitely enjoyed the aftermath!

One day, as we played about along the road that passed near our village, I learned something I might probably never otherwise have come to know. I was born at a time when the people in the village were rather proud of being 'saved'. Many had become Christians and were developing growing disdain for customs that were 'native'. As some women passed us on their way to the fields, we heard one of them saying to the others that a certain village woman was no longer putting on a kerchief.

'I know she is going back to the dark and will be owned by Satan shortly,' the woman declared.

'Why do you say others are going to the dark,' another said, 'while you still take snuff, though in secrecy? You thought we did not know? It would be better if you piled your own firewood first before helping others get wood to burn themselves.'

2.

Boys Will Be Boys

One cold and cloudy afternoon three of us small boys were roasting maize in my grandmother's hut. The fire was excellent, the old woman having preserved the driest and best wood for the cold season. Granny was there too to help us roast the maize, though she would only watch as we argued as to who would take which part of the cob when dividing it into three parts. Among the three of us, I was the only first-born and, according to children's tradition, I was to take the head portion of the cob. This was normally not well roasted and I objected several times. Paulo, being neither first-born nor last-born, claimed the middle portion, declaring that he came in the middle among his mother's children. The third boy was the last-born among us, so the bottom portion was supposed to be his. Like the head portion, the bottom part had some maize raw or over-roasted. And like me the boy complained. It was firm advice from our grandmother that settled it.

'The child who comes first from his mother's womb must always eat the portion of the maize-cob which is born first,' she reminded us. 'And the last-born baby should take the bottom portion, because it develops last from the womb of the maize stalk. Does every one of you understand that? Now I don't want to hear you argue.'

When the fire started to clear out, Granny became reluctant to let us use more firewood.

'Stand up and go out! How much firewood have *you* brought into this house?' she would ask, directing the words to any one of us.

After some time, Granny removed the nice burning stumps and poured water on them, to our utter surprise and disappointment. For there was still a basket half-full of maize cobs.

'When the red charcoal no longer smoulders, I want all of you out or I pinch your thighs. You should be playing outside.' She spoke with her peculiar way of pronouncing words.

Paulo's sister came in just as we were wondering what to do next. The fire was almost gone, Granny having scratched the greater portion of the charcoal to her side of the fireplace.

'If I tell you something, will you believe me?' the girl asked, eyes shining.

'And hear her!' cried Granny. 'How can a girl like you make such a statement? When you want to say something, you don't ask people if they will believe what you tell them. Tell us now.'

'The white cow is giving birth,' the girl informed us.

We all knew the animal she meant. There was one white cow, and anyway a woman had recently said she could give birth any day.

'Let us go and see,' Paulo suggested.

'Yes, let us go,' I said.

'Eee, so when you hear one of your mothers is giving birth you will want to go and see. No? Your mothers are not cows? Never think of it any day. Go! I am even sick of having you here.' Granny scolded.

We dashed out of the hut. When we came to the enclosure where the cow was said to be lying, we met two village women and some children.

'*Ajai!* Look at these boys! Are you girls to be watching a cow giving birth?' one woman asked.

We knew she meant it was bad for us. As men, we were not supposed to be present where a female gave birth. The woman only intended to teach us the day-to-day manners. When some boys and even girls laughed at the sight of the cow in pain, we were ordered away at once. So we never witnessed the end.

This disappointed us. But as with other children there were always many things around to occupy us. It was cold, and running about wouldn't be so bad after all. A game of touch was started. We were several now and the nearest house was my aunt's. This and the food stores around made large enough objects to be rounded at full speed. One boy would touch another and run away. The touched boy, if tricky, might pretend to chase the attacker and then stop, the escaping boy continuing to run round the house unaware that he was not being chased. Then he would suddenly appear from the other direction to find his supposed chaser in readiness to touch him and pass back Bad Omen. Of course the escaping, panting boy would be startled, not knowing whether to turn back and run or to yield and, in the confusion, might stagger and fall, laughing uncontrollably, probably to mask some weakness. The attacker would then touch him several times and run off before the laugher could regain control.

'Now, it is done, don't allow him to touch you! He will sleep among devils this night,' we would say and laugh loudly and mockingly in the direction of the last boy to bear the devilish traces.

Unfortunately for us, we had not known there was a baby sleeping in the house. She burst out crying and the nurse-sibling reproached us as the cause.

'No, I don't think the playing boys woke up the baby. You did not feed her properly,' said the mother when she came, to the nurse. 'You must always know that a baby cries when it is sick or has an empty stomach. When she cries again, feed her.'

The mother dropped the bundle of firewood she had brought. Then asking for a stool, she summoned her daughter, the nurse, to bring the baby who had fallen back to sleep, probably tired from prolonged crying. The baby had cried for such a long time that the nurse despaired, perhaps, that the little creature would ever keep silent. She had stopped the lullabies which we had helped her sing.

A stool was brought and Aunt sat down and prepared to breast-feed her baby. She asked for water in a basin, adding that the baby was not only hungry but had to be washed. The water was brought, the small baby was dipped into the basin and the woman's hands sprinkled water on the baby. The water must have been cold for the baby, awake, went on crying loudly.

'Do not cry! Keep quiet, or you will not finish the milk in my breasts!' the woman said to the baby. As if the little maid could understand a word! Then holding the baby securely in her hands, the woman stood, and tossed her up and down, up and down. After swinging her sideways several times, she sat down on the stool, and spreading an old towel over her closed thighs, she laid the baby astride, covering her with the towel to dry. My aunt mumbled some comforting words as the feeding proceeded.

When the baby had suckled the two breasts, the woman examined the small child's belly and said, 'This daughter of mine is still hungry. One of you should go and bring me the porridge and I will see if she will eat some.'

Paulo ran inside and brought a small gourd that contained some porridge made from maize flour. This the woman gave to the baby, using her finger and at times a small spoon. The baby, who had just started to crawl, was reluctant to take porridge. When we laughed, my aunt rebuked us, saying we were interfering with the baby's feeding.

'Go away, you boys. You cannot even give the baby a chance to eat peacefully! Or do *you* want the porridge? All right, take it and share it among yourselves.'

We were just bigger babies who, therefore, could feed ourselves, that's all. There were four of us. We pulled out the porridge by turns from the gourd. When some little porridge was remaining, it was left to Paulo who, although the oldest, was the smallest of the four. We always deemed him the child among us. He complained at this treatment in spite of the fact that he always got the best part of everything as a child. Like the grownups, we knew that 'the child' must always have preference in food and all other things.

One day Paulo's mother and my mother were planning to go to the market. Paulo and I were to be left to nurse his baby sister. Before the women went, the baby was securely placed on Paulo's back, being held there by a support made from ox-hide. This was tied round his waist and hung over the head. The baby was placed on Paulo's back so that when the support was hanging she would be in a sitting position, one leg hanging loosely at either side.

'When the baby cries, shake her as you move around the house singing lullabies,' one woman said to Paulo.

'And you,' she said to me, 'pat the baby on the back through the support and sing:

> Keep quiet, baby,
> And keep quiet, baby!
> Your mother is there.
> She is there, coming,
> Coming to suckle you.
> Keep quiet baby!

Do you hear that? I don't want you to remove the baby, Paulo. You might both fall to the ground.'

It appeared as if Paulo was about to go on strike, after thinking over the whole process.

'No, I will not be left with the baby,' said he, threatening to unhook the support from his head.

'Eee! Can you really refuse to carry the baby?' his mother asked, 'when I am going to bring you sugar canes, oranges, bananas, guavas, brown sugar, sweets, and all?'

'Don't forget to bring me lemons and a piece of sugar cane,' I reminded my mother. I always loved eating bitter fruit.

For the greater part of the afternoon, we sat in the shade on the verandah of the hut. Paulo was seated on a stool, for with a baby on his back he could not sit flat on the ground with comfort. We kept ourselves busy with all sorts of occupations such as play-cooking in mud dishes, being hosts to imaginary people, drawing sketches of the huts and animals in the soil. The baby was very co-operative and slept meanwhile. However, when we heard the rumble of a motor vehicle, we could not restrain ourselves. We ran towards the road to see. In our scramble to get there in time, the baby woke up and started to cry. We did as our mothers had instructed, but all in vain. Our lullabies had no effect on the baby. At last Paulo gave up and started to cry. I tried to persuade him not to cry but, when I failed, burst out crying, too. We continued to cry until our mothers came home. The women knew how to keep us quiet, though. They gave us sugar canes, and promised never to leave us with that naughty girl again.

3.

Thorns in the Grass

As time passed by, we would boast about how we young boys were growing up together in the village, advancing in age and size. Bad Omen continued to be a favourite game of our play group and village for years. As I have already said, any number of children of any age could and did play. If all the children were from the same small village, the game was usually played on an inter-home basis. If the number of players was small, even two such as Paulo and me, Bad Omen could at any moment be declared transmittable. But it was when the group was made up of children from different villages that the game became thrilling. Members from one village would try to pass Bad Omen to the members of the other village, who formed a united front to avoid having one of their number be touched last and thus have to take Bad Omen home with him. They knew they would be visited by evil spirits if he did, and nightmares would befall all of them.

'Take and bear all, for my father, my brothers and sisters, all the people from my village!' each pursuer would say to the attacked, making sure that he himself stayed clear of any opponent. This chasing and being chased would continue through the late afternoon and far beyond sunset. When it grew too dark to give chase any longer and the game had to stop, the children from one village or the other would very gravely turn homeward, bearing Bad Omen. There was never any question of a draw.

Passing Bad Omen was not played on land only. We frequently played it in a natural swimming pool that would form in a stream during the rains, and persist for only short periods afterwards. The pool would be full of boulders and thorny branches collected from distant hills, stacked along the banks, and then scattered all over the pool. In the middle the current was strong and fast. A child could easily be carried down stream with no hope of return, if we were not careful. Though the water was muddy, the sandy banks formed a sort of resort place for children from the villages around. Boys and girls of various ages, from about seven to fifteen, would gather here for a swim.

Inside the pool, we would play Bad Omen. The attacker

would dive towards his target, the rule being that Bad Omen could be passed only if the attacker was travelling under water. The boy or girl being chased would also dive to avoid the attacker and, if lucky, get away to the far end of the pool. It was not unusual to find boys coming up out of the water, their faces plastered with mud after hitting the banks or, having landed on a thorny branch, declaring that they would never swim again.

When one team learned that it was about to be defeated, the game in the pool might very well turn into a war. Here fighting was not done with the hands. One of us would jump high and swirl into a dive, hitting his opponent with the legs. This was most exciting to those watching from the banks, but not so pleasant for the players, especially the smaller ones who in many cases ended up crying.

Drying ourselves on the sandy banks, we would think up more leisurely games. We would cover ourselves with sand up to our heads, for example, pretending to be dead and buried. We would model clay toys, such as motor cars and various domestic animals. These we would take home with us in the evening while driving back the few *real* domestic animals that we had been looking after.

Another favourite play spot was the sweet potato field. Here all of us, boys and girls alike, would dig up the sweet potatoes. Then using soft lumps of soil, we would build a conical kiln over a small round hole we had dug in the ground. This kiln we would fire, until the red-hot lumps could roast the sweet roots. It was not a simple matter to build a successful kiln. It could so easily collapse while being fired, as the soil lumps would soften with the heat. Nevertheless, strange things were associated with any boy or girl who, having commented on the beauty of a kiln, would see it collapse. Such a person was said to belong to a group of people who by nature had evil in their blood and so, by mere comment could spoil anything.

Digging up sweet potatoes and roasting them in kilns not only provided food for us children to eat. We were also learning to work together in co-operation. Those who did not take part in digging up the sweet roots, picking up suitable lumps of soil or rubbish for firing, were not allowed to partake of the roasted potatoes. There was frequently a nice lesson for the older, stronger, but unco-operative child in the general process of making the sweet roots edible. I remember an incident that occurred when a certain boy was reluctant to participate in making a kiln. He probably did not mean to refuse, for he was doing high jump at the time, which apparently absorbed him fully. In any case, the potatoes were roasted and ready for consumption by the time the poor boy arrived, hungry. He was therefore sent away to round up some cows. He could not refuse for there was still hope that he would get a share. However in his absence the potatoes were devoured completely. Then at the smart suggestion of an older child we put some human faeces where the potatoes had been and covered them up with the hot soil. We moved aside, under command of the oldest boy, and took an oath.

'We shall keep quiet!' ordered the boy, after which we declared: 'We tie our tongues and maintain silence completely and fully!'

Everyone knew what to expect. This was not the first time such a thing had happened, nor the second. Always the unco-operative boy would come dashing back after rounding up the cows.

'And are you not going now to give me some potatoes?' the boy asked on returning.

The one in command gave answer that we had been waiting for him, all of us willing to give him the honour of sharing the potatoes, even though he had not helped with the earlier jobs.

By this time the soil would be cool enough and the boy, feeling with his fingers the part where he had seen the potatoes buried, eagerly scratched to get at the tasty food. We dared not laugh at all, any of us, lest breaking the oath would kill us or the older boys knock our faces with their knuckles. So we just watched, watched till the poor fellow had his fingers stuck in the faeces. Then we laughed 'till our ribs stretched,' as we always said, much to the shame of the boy but quite to the amusement of the rest of us, who were soon rolling on the ground with laughter. So the boy was taught a good lesson. We had no doubt that next time he would co-operate or build his own kiln.

Harvesting season, and the removal of foodstuffs from the fields, would bring to us children a long period of play and great satisfaction. Instead of going to herd the cows far away, we could now let them roam about in the nearby fields. This freedom and leisure were wonderful for all of us. Such periods would normally begin early in the month of August, extending perhaps till late in September, when the adults would again start uncovering the water-furrows and ploughing in readiness for sowing. Then back we would go, reluctantly, to the usual herding in the distant fields. This would bring once more the inconvenience, but also the fascination, of having to examine all the patches on our clothes, as we looked for lice. These lice, we believed, when buried alive, would hasten the setting of the sun. After burying whatever lice we could find, we would watch the shade on a nearby hill and, seeing it rush to the west, would imagine the sun to be sinking faster and faster. We knew it would travel quickly beneath the earth while we slept, to appear on the eastern horizon next morning in time to stop the shade. Then, if we wanted the morning sun to stay shining longer in the sky, we would build an image to her, using green stalks of grass, and sing:

> Sun, do shine,
> And I'll make you an ornament,
> An ornament of five layers.

If it began to drizzle and we would get wet, we would praise the sun and ask her to chase the shadows as we sang:

> Sun, chase the shade,
> So that my clothes will dry!

This song we would sing in a serious manner until the sun really did shine again.

For many days, I remember, we used to play at the junction of the village path and the wide foot-path which passed near the village. This at times became a motor track, but only on exceptional occasions, such as when a certain Sergeant-Major of the old Army would return home. One rainy evening the Sergeant-Major was returning, when his heavy truck got stuck at our play spot. Several villagers gathered to help him. To remove the large vehicle they cut branches off trees, uprooted sisal plants, and placed these under the wheels. At last the lorry managed to travel up the track. But it left deep ruts and a spoiled play spot. We had to shift our play to another part of the foot-path.

This gave some boys from a nearby village the opportunity to play along the small banks of our old play spot. After playing there for some time, they left one day, but not until they had dropped their faeces all up and down the banks.

Towards evening a smart villager, on leave, happened to pass near the junction. Having stayed in a town as a *toto* to an Indian, and classifying himself among those who were already Europeanized, he became thoroughly disgusted at seeing the faeces the boys had dropped along the way. Indeed, he spared the time to go round the whole village to warn our mothers.

'You woman,' said the smart fellow when he came to our house, 'you try and tell your kid where to drop his faeces. Otherwise his buttocks will swell with sticks!'

'And what is wrong?' asked my mother.

'I have said already. I am not a sheep to bleat back what I have said.' And with that, he hurried off.

His threats had been quite unnecessary. Our mothers had taught us to get rid of faeces in the bushes far from the paths. The older boys and girls had told us the same thing. We would even reproach one another for any attempt to empty our bowels near the paths. With urinating it was another matter. Nobody cared, provided we were outside the house.

These habits were among the many things we had come to learn as a result of constant telling by the women and older children. Our fathers seldom took part in such 'training,' which included increasing knowledge of our close and distant relatives, respect for the adults, especially the aged, sex education in a limited sense, and ways of dealing with strangers. The older children, boys in particular, would often argue with us as to whom a certain child belonged. They knew that with the Kamba a child was identified first with the father and finally with the mother. A drunk father might ask his young child the same questions daily, 'You! To whom do you belong? And who is your paternal grandfather? Eh, and who is your mother?' until the boy could answer quickly and confidently. In sex education the emphasis was on training the girls especially. Mothers were very strict as to how the small girls should sit. A girl was always to sit with the thighs together and the dress pulled over the knees. If a stranger greeted us, we were to reply politely. If he gave us something edible, we were to hold it till he was out of sight, then throw it away. Anything given by strangers could cause us harm, we were told, and witchcraft was common.

There were other lessons in safety, I remember, especially for the smaller ones, for the environment of our childhood was vested with dangers without number. There was the fire, with the pot placed on three stones, perhaps steaming heavily as the meal was being cooked. I recall particularly the porridge cooking, with those shooting drops, as the meal boiled and we all sat round the fireplace in expectation of a tasty meal. We always got the same warnings, whether in my grandmother's hut, my mother's house, or my aunt's. If we played too close to the fireplace, one of the women would tell us, 'You will be burned. Fear this!' and she would point to the fire.

At times my grandmother would, I suppose, pretend to have been burned, for she would turn aside, wriggling as if in pain. This would make us laugh, and retreat to the door as well.

'Did you see that? Are you not witnesses now?' Grandma would say, resuming her former position and continuing to stir the boiling porridge, prepared from sorghum, millet flour or maize.

When we would move close to the fire she never failed to give warning: 'Did you not see me being burned a few moments ago? If I, a grown woman, can be burned, how about you, a child as you are?' This would be said in pretence of tremendous seriousness.

'Don't old women get wounds when they are burned?' Paulo wanted to know.

Perhaps this question defeated our grandmother momentarily. She ordered us out, saying we were warming ourselves when we should have been playing. We obeyed, dashing out, only to be ordered back into the hut by a village old man.

'Return to your mothers now!' the old man shouted. 'The black cow is leading the cattle! If she finds you here in her path you will be trodden before you realize what is happening.'

The black cow was famous. She would spare her horns on no child or dog in front of her. This we knew and we rushed back to the hut of our grandmother.

'And you boys,' Granny roared. 'Did I not tell you to go and play outside?'

'But we were told that the black cow is coming!' one of us said.

'Yes, stay then. Those horns can break your backs. Always play outside when the cows are away. When they come back, take refuge inside the buildings.'

Indeed, it appeared that dangers of one sort or another lurked all round the village. There were the half-wild bulls, and the sheep and the goats, which could tread mercilessly on a helpless child. There were thorns in the wild grasses where we played hide-and-seek and, of course, all the insects, which grown-ups used to tell us were animals.

In those days, too, there was a story on the tongues of everyone in the village about how So-and-So had disappeared underground while running in chase across a certain field. The truth was that the unfortunate fellow had dropped into an old latrine-pit, which had been dug two years previously. The grass had grown over the top and, since the person who dug it had gone off job-hunting, no one had bothered to build the latrine. The poor fellow who was said to have disappeared had obviously plunged into the hole while his chasing friend had stopped to extract a thorn. When the chaser looked around after a short time, he could not see his friend anywhere across the field. He called out again and again, but meeting with no success, he went along home. On arriving, he found that his friend was not there either. So for three days the unfortunate fellow lay groaning deep in the dark bottom of the pit. Then he was found on sheer chance by a herdsboy. Had it not been for one of his cows, who feared the hole, and thus led the herdsboy to examine the area to see what had startled the cow, the man would most surely have died in the hole. But on hearing the poor fellow groan, the boy ran to break the news to the villagers, and the rescue was made.

This was the story, although not the version that was told to us children. I only happened to pick it up several years later. In order to keep our play group away from the vicious thorns, the insects, and the snakes of the field, the mothers, trying to frighten us, had said that we too could disappear underground.

I should have said that the girls would take part in some though not all of our childhood play. Especially in their imitative play, the girls would fashion their activities more within the limits of the routine work done by women. They would cook food, for example, from soil mixed with water or urine. They would gather wood and nurse children, these children being anything from maize-cobs or small gourds to bundles of clothes. Some girls liked to accompany their mothers or elder sisters to the well to get water, to the bush to fetch firewood, to the fields to get food for the evening meal. In short, the girls became more and more feminine in their choice of play, which was really the beginning of their work.

With the boys, it was different. We could and did play what the girls played and, in addition, played what any girl would have been rebuked for if found doing. Such boys' play included head-standing, forward-rolling, wrestling, and walking on the hands. Riding three-wheeled toy carts down steep slopes, and hunting birds and small animals like the hare were also regarded as masculine occupations rather than feminine.

4.
Circumcision Without Ceremony

It was August of 1949, a dry month, and also the season for circumcision. I was hardly seven at the time. One morning my aunt came to our home, accompanied by a cousin of mine, a girl. She was older than I by about four rainy seasons which, translated in my place, would make about two years. Nevertheless we were of the same 'age group'. I had been waiting for them to come for I knew we were to go for circumcision. Though the purpose and meaning, even the nature, of circumcision were very vague to us, we both desired it. We knew it would mean the end of the mockery we had been receiving from boys and girls on the way to and from the primary school we had attended for about eight months. In fact, some four older boys had recently forced my shorts open to witness that I had not been circumcised. Then they had laughed loudly and called me an 'uncircumcised'.

This came to my mind now as we walked the one mile's distance to the place of the ceremony. I had left my shorts behind and only the shirt was there to do battle with nakedness. When we arrived at our destination, there were many other children, boys and girls of our own ages. The girls were crowded together in one group and the boys in another. I joined my group and my aunt led my cousin to hers. Several middle-aged men and women kept the groups separate and the members close together.

'He who cries during circumcision is a woman, not a man,' said one fellow, sniffing hesitantly as a result of strong snuff.

'By the justice of God I will not cry,' the boys whispered among themselves.

There did not seem to be much talking among the women, I noticed. Maybe they were frightened. Then I realized it would hardly be appropriate for their guards to take courage and say, 'She who cries is not a woman but a man.'

The sun was climbing rapidly overhead. The party we had been waiting for arrived at last. This was an elderly man and woman in the company of several younger men. The old man was clad in an old grey-to-black heavy blanket and on his head was a fez. The woman wore black calico, topped by a brightly-coloured red-and-white-striped shawl. She had bangles on her wrists and carried a fly whisk in her left hand. A shiny foot-long metal tube, serving as a snuff store, dangled from her waist; all of this made her reminiscent of a real sorceress. The small group disappeared behind the huts. Soon after, a girl and boy at the same time, turn by turn, would be led away in the same direction. Nor did they ever come back again, which increased the suspense and anxiety. We knew they had gone to be circumcised, but that was all. How it was actually done remained a puzzle only to be solved when we ourselves would be taken beyond those huts.

When my turn came, it was also the turn of an older girl whom I had seen at times passing by our village. We were taken beyond the huts to find two groups of men and women separated by a thin bush. In my group a very muscular man, who I am sure was suffering from elephantiasis, was sitting with his legs wide apart, the dry grass between them now all red with blood. This was for me the first time to see so much wasted human blood. Its appearance shook my courage greatly. The old man was unwrapping a knife, which had been tied in a white cloth. Another fellow was sharpening a knife near the women. I was told to sit down in front of the muscular man, in the manner in which he was seated. I obeyed, and the big man lifted my legs, placing them on his own and twisting them under, so that when he moved his huge legs aside, mine were clamped tight. He then placed his great hands round my belly. Two more men stood behind us, one holding my hands behind the big man. I looked straight forward, but I knew there was blood. Yes, and the old man was approaching, crouched down with that glittering knife. Fear engulfed me. Then my head was turned sideways. The elephantiasis man moved his legs outwards, further tightening the grip on my legs and belly. I was terrified.

I felt the rough, cold fingers of the old man touch and explore my private parts as if he was taking measure. The thought of crying came to me. But it was no use. Before I could open my mouth, it was all over. And I was being led to a circular hut, the blood dripping from my wound.

In the hut were other boys who had undergone the process before me. Their wounds were not bleeding now; the blood had clotted. I squatted down among them. Mine soon stopped bleeding also. There was no pain at first, I remember. Pain was to come later, when the sun was highest in the sky and the horizon bubbled with heat. Later on, I learned that the girls had been held just as tight as we had. But immediately after the old woman had circumcised them, the girls had been set to forced hopping, perhaps to help drain the blood, I don't know. It was a tall woman, we were told, who would force the circumcised girls in their turn to jump up. Some cried out as if in enormous pain. It seemed as if the process was harder on them than on us. We could hear the one foot of one of the girls pounding on the ground even as we sat inside the house. Another time, when one of them was forced to hop, we could hear her land on the ground with unstable legs, emitting a sharp cry of pain.

When evening came and the great heat had subsided, we all walked home, a journey which was not easy. Because our wounds forced us to walk with legs apart, it came to be known to whoever we met that we had been circumcised. I made short steps, I recall, but the girls' steps were shorter still. I could tell from the way they walked that at least I was better off. Circumcision for girls was real torture. Blessed be the changes that, through the intervening years in my tribe, have brought about the complete disappearance of female circum-cision.

Not so with male circumcision. Every Kamba father insists that his young son be circumcised. He will give no good reason for it when asked. 'I was circumcised. So was my father before me,' he will say, 'and his father and father's father before him.' At one time, many years back, there was a kind of traditional initiation ceremony in our place that followed years after the circumcision. But this is no more. Only the circumcision itself, quite without ceremony, persists to this day.

The healing of our wounds, I should say, was miraculous. No medicine powders were used at all. Nature and dust seemed to take care of everything. Some older boys had warned me that if I washed my wound with soap, it would never heal and, respecting their experience, I followed the advice. They also told me to go to the hillside to the blue lizards' abode, collect their droppings and, after crushing these into powder, apply the powder to my wound, using saliva as the adhesive. This they said would accelerate the recovery. It sounded likely. But when I began to imagine myself collecting such medicine on the cliffs near our village, where the wind was so strong as to blow a person's hat up the hillside or down to the foot of the preci-pitous rocks below, fear overcame me. I was sure to trip while looking for the medicinal droppings, I told myself, and then I would disappear down the cliffs into eternity.

As it was, the wound did all right. We played in the gardens, built kilns for roasting the sweet potatoes, as usual, and thus soiled the wounds. Within three weeks I could put on my shorts and go back to school. I was in Class A now. The 'big one', the teachers called it—Standard I A, I suppose.

5.

I Go to School

The idea of starting school was very thrilling to me. I did not quite know why I wanted to go. Perhaps it was because my mother had urged me, and the other children too were going.

We started Primary School at eight o'clock on a January morning in 1949, but there was no 'learning' that day. The school had first to be cleaned after a month of negligence. The paths were all overgrown with grass. Some desks were missing after a theft at Christmas-time which had been talked of by everyone. The mud walled reed-thatched classrooms appeared to have but a few days to stand, the buildings leaning far to the west. But while no one dared forecast just when they would topple down, the stubborn old structures stood firm, the grass grown up to their very doors.

Some of the bigger boys of the school were set to clearing the paths, with *jembes* and *pangas* that they had been detailed to bring to school before leaving for the Christmas holiday. Others weeded the small but important school garden. We smaller boys collected the cut grass and carried it to a compost heap a few hundred steps away. The teacher, a medium-sized, middle-aged person in a smart khaki suit, wearing shoes with heels badly worn off at the sides, I remember, kept looking sternly at us. I did not like the way he swung that bamboo stick. It would whiz through the air and sound very terrifying.

'That is Moses, who struck a boy dead at the school of Cold Waters,' whispered one small boy. 'I think . . .'

'You lie,' interrupted another. 'He is called Kamanzi. I know him for he comes from near my home. He has been teaching at the Africa Inland Mission School. They say he knows how to use the stick.' This boy was probably right.

The teacher, watching us, spoke at last. 'Do not just stand! (to the bigger boys). And you (to us, the small ones), you carry much grass and run like hares, or else this cane will tell you what to do!'

The warning was obeyed by everyone. The big boys dared not stand. We, the small ones, collected the grass and rushed it to the heap. It was a wild sort of commotion, I remember, that running and throwing of grass, with soil still attached to the roots. The air round the compost heap became dusty and we had to close our eyes near that place. One boy failed to do so and dust particles entered his eyes. He lingered behind a moment, rubbing his eyes.

'Wee, wee, wee! Come here quickly,' shouted the teacher.

The boy hastened towards him, still rubbing his eyes. He reached the fierce and angry master to be caught at the nape of the neck with his big left hand. The poor child was pushed forward and, the teacher having raised his left leg so ingeniously, rested on the teacher's thigh. He wriggled about as the stick smarted this part and that of the buttocks. When the boy was released, his eyes were small springs of tears. From his mouth came a deafening wail.

'Idiot! Silly! Awkward! What on earth! Small little thing thinks mother is here and school is home!' mocked the teacher. 'Shut up now! Otherwise . . . . .'

The boy stopped crying at once.

'Did you feel that?'

'Ye-es.'

'Yes what?' asked the teacher.

'Yes, *Muvea*.'

'You small rat, I am not a *Muvea*! I am a *Mwalimu*,' thundered the man. 'Do you hear that? Do you hear that?' he asked again.

'Yes, *Mwalimu*.'

The attention of all of us was focused on the poor child who thought everyone at the Catholic School was a *Muvea*. We had stopped carrying grass to watch, but the enraged teacher did not see us. As he turned our way we got moving.

The cleaning of the compound continued for about a week. After cutting grass every day, we played at random on the play-ground. The older boys of the school would tease us, claiming they had to welcome and open the school with us. They kicked at and pinched the newcomers, though not all the new boys were touched. (I was among the latter, the 'smart' ones. Perhaps they thought a smart boy came from a rich family and hence had powerful parents. Those boys in tattered clothes and without shorts really had it the hard way.) After playing, we would go to the classrooms and be taught songs, leaving the school at midday.

When learning really started, I thought it was wonderful, though fear reigned within the mud walls. The teacher would come in with some books and, of course, a stick. The first day

we made a mistake for which we were severely punished. We
failed to stand up when the master entered.

'Where have you been harvested?' snapped the man.

Silence.

'Stand! Sit! Stand! Sit!' commanded the teacher.

There was as yet no rhythm in the buttocks' striking the
desks and this seemed to annoy him more. He snatched his
stick and with a swift start struck us all on our heads, which
had been shaved clean in preparation for starting school. He
went to every pupil in the class. Then once again:

'Stand! Sit! Stand! Sit!' There was rhythm now, and satisfaction for the teacher.

'When I come in, you stand up till I say 'Sit!!' the teacher
reminded us. Next he took down all our names.

'What is your name?' he asked the first boy.

'My name is Mutua, son of Mulwa, Teacher.' He took the
name of each of us in turn, then started our first lesson on the
board. The blackboard was lined, I remember, and he slowly
shaped the vowels on it. Then he began:

Teacher: 'A.'

Pupils: 'A-ee.'

Teacher: 'E.'

Pupils: 'E-ee.'

And so on till a bell was rung. A lady teacher entered as the
man left, carrying on with the same stern philosophy.

'Stand! Sit! Stand! Sit!' And she walked around the room
to catch those who did not obey. Then she shaped the numbers
on the board, 0 to 9, and we sang as instructed.

Teacher: 'One.'

Pupils: 'One.'

Teacher: 'Two.'

Pupils: 'Two-oo.'

On and on, with many repetitions, till that period ended.

For a week or two we did nothing but sing the vowels and
the numerals after the teachers. When we had mastered them
fully by sound, we were lined up outside the school to shape
them on the ground. The next stage was to write the letters
on slates. Within the course of the year we had mastered the
vowels and the rest of the alphabet, and the numerals. By the
end of the year, we were writing words and doing simple
addition and subtraction. We had also learned some simple
prayers. Good stories about the Child Jesus, together with a

description of the benefits of Heaven and the horrors of Hell, took pride of place in the classroom. The old man who taught us Religion spoke with a great confidence, as if he had actually been to Nazareth, Heaven and Hell. He made us liken Heaven to the place of the European and the rich, where good food, nice clothes, beautiful houses, motor cars and servants would be at our disposal.

'You will get everything, everything you can think of,' this teacher would promise.

'Even motor cars and servants?' one boy asked in great wonder.

'Small fool!' shouted the old man, 'When I say everything, it means all things you will ask for. You will just tell an angel what you want and it will be brought to you ... But in Hell, in Hell misery will be plentiful. Lucifer will be there to welcome you with red hot charcoal. When you say *Hodi*, he will open the door. And as you gape in wonder at the awful sight, he will throw red hot charcoal into your mouth. Do you hear that, small ones?'

'Yes, Teacher,' the pupils would reply, filled with fear at the very thought of such a place.

Then he would show us the portraits of Child Jesus and Mary, and the picture of Heaven, with people singing to God at the centre and under them Hell. The devil, Lucifer, was black with horns, and with snakes twisted round his body.

'Look at these snakes! Did I not tell you that there is horror in Hell? Look at Lucifer!'

Then the bell would ring and the period ended. And so, in time, did our first year.

The second year of Primary School brought with it more writing, reading, arithmetic, handwork, and more stories of Heaven and Hell. Religion was taken more seriously now. On Monday mornings before classes started, Father Layton would come round with a stick, to punish the little *shenzis* who had not attended the Holy Mass. He would enter a classroom and, in accordance with the custom of the school, all pupils would stand.

'How are you, Father?' the pupils would greet him.

'I am quite well,' Father Layton would reply.

Then silence till the *Mzungu* said, 'Sit!' The teacher in the classroom had no authority.

Not everybody would sit down. Those who had failed to attend Mass were left standing. This was how we had been trained by our teacher, *Mwalimu* Paulana. He always told us, 'God is everywhere and sees you when you tell a lie.'

'Are these the *shenzis*, *Mwalimu*?'

'Yes, Father,' the trembling *Mwalimu* Paulana would say.

Then the offenders would be caned in front of us, after which the *Muvea* would move on to the next classroom to execute this Monday morning's engagement. Some of the boys cried. Others became indignant as *Mwalimu* Paulana started the religious period. We were told about the Faith, taught the so-called truths about the Faith. But still, to some of us, there remained room for doubt that the Faith was taught us in the proper way.

Yet I loved learning, in spite of the fear. The third and fourth years of Primary School came and went. Swahili, English, General Knowledge, were among the new subjects. We had covered the multiplication tables, long division and multiplication by the end of the third year. Everyone was eager to learn Swahili to 'ask for water from the Indians', and English to ask for employment from the *Mzungu*, when the need should arise. By the end of the fourth year I could answer greetings in Swahili and English. I also knew quite a number of words, but could not coordinate them into sentences.

Of all the teaching staff in the Primary School, as I look back on it now, Mutunga and Kekiyu were perhaps the most interesting characters. Like all the others, they trembled when they talked to the *Muvea*. This *Muvea* was small in stature but very commanding. His presence would reduce the teachers to the stature of slaves. However, once away from the *Muvea*, Mutunga and Kekiyu would suddenly change and begin cursing.

'Does he think his mother is older than mine? Did he not find me here when he came? And now because he is a *Mzungu*, he will abuse me as if I am a boy!' We heard Mutunga say this one day, right after a thorough scorching from the *Muvea*. He had been found teaching arithmetic in a period that was meant for religion. We all sympathized with Mutunga. He worked hard and wanted all of us to pass the Competitive Common Entrance Examination. This made him deal with the buttocks harshly. He was a 'professional' at caning.

Kekiyu was another character, whom we hated and liked in turn. We knew he did not teach Nature Study well, and he boasted too much. He too would beat us often, sometimes quite unjustifiably, and call us bad names when he came to the classroom. But he told us interesting stories about the war in

Burma, Abyssinia, and even in Garissa, Kenya. He taught us the songs they used to sing as soldiers overseas, fighting a war the causes of which they knew nothing.

The songs ran something like this, I remember:

> Hitler is a bad club,
> He has destroyed Europe.
> Hitler is an ugly club.
> Hitler, Hitla-la-a,
> Hitler has no *Kipande*.
>
> Man never dies unless God so wishes.
> I saw this on board to Burma.
> The ship was bombed now and again,
> Yet she sailed like the wind.

Mwalimu Kekiyu would often interrupt his lessons with such songs, which we sang with joy. He very much liked the rainy seasons. Whenever it started raining, and the raindrops came straight in through the bare patches of the thatch, we would crowd into one corner of the classroom. Here we would all start singing the war songs, and *Mwalimu* would be the happier for it. Unlike the Headmaster, who made us sing the boring Church songs, *Mwalimu* Kekiyu always gave us something to suit our taste.

The Competitive Common Entrance Examination came at the end of the fourth year, eliminating from further education the larger number of my classmates. These boys were never to taste of the Intermediate School, which directly followed Primary Four. Instead of going to read in those fine stone, iron-roofed classrooms with cement floors, they were now to be swallowed up by the waiting coffee estates of the 'settlers' around Ol Doinyo Sabuk. The small *Muvea*, who was then Father-in-Charge of the Mission, helped by his loyal Headmaster, had already warned us that many were old enough to go to work somewhere. And this was true. Some of the boys of P4 already had beards beginning to show.

6.
Mistrust and Punishment

When the results of the Competitive Common Entrance Examination came, I found myself among the winners in the competition for Standard Five. The examination had been no problem. I entered the Intermediate School on merit.

From the Primary School I came with Bernard, among others, who for long remained a friend. *Mwalimu* Leo had been promoted from Primary to teach the Intermediate. But he seemed to make little use of what he had learned during a refresher course of which he boasted prior to the promotion. Instead he went on with the same old ways of forcing us to learn things instead of helping and directing our learning. This man, aided by a leather whip, made us cram and memorize Rural Science notes. The Catechism and St. Mark's Gospel were memorized too. If anyone left out as much as an article he was whipped. One day my friend Bernard was badly thrashed because he could not define 'irrigation,' word for word from his notes.

Father Magill, who at times posed as Headmaster and at other times talked of *Mwalimu* Nzyoka as 'the boss', was also a constant threat. Here as in the Primary School, English, Swahili, History, Geography, Rural Science, Arithmetic, and Handwork all came after Religion. When we went to school at eight, we had first to go to the Church and say our morning prayers. (Father Magill always told us he knew we became little *shenzis* at home.) Class periods started and ended with a prayer and, before we left, we said the evening prayers. Those who dared run away from the prayers were severely dealt with.

It was Father Magill now who, before the classes started on Monday mornings, had the duty to execute. He had a special cane in his office for punishing those who had not attended Mass. Only now this *Muvea* carried on some spiritual segregation. The unbaptized pagan *shenzis* were indiscriminately packed together to be 'converted' by *Mwalimu* Leo, while Father Magill would take the more fortunate baptized ones. I was among these, for I had been baptized in childhood with only my mother's consent. Father Magill taught us how to confess our sins and receive the Holy Communion. When he gave us permission to go to confession and Holy Communion, we were delighted.

In the meantime, the pagans were being taught the catechism in preparation for Baptism and cleansing.

At the end of the second year in the Intermediate School, I came out as the best pupil in the overall end-of-year tests. Father Magill had promised to offer prizes to the best pupil in each of the four classes. The prizes were very boyish, that for my class being a tennis ball. Pupils from the other classes received their prizes, but I never got mine. This was the story. One Thursday evening, the day before the school was to close for the holiday, we were told to go and confess our sins. I joined the other boys and told Father Magill my sins. They were simple. I could have mentioned them to any friend. One, I had refused to attend Mass, through laziness. Two, I had not said my morning prayers for three days. And three, I had lied to an adult. This adult was a relative of mine who had sent me somewhere on an errand. As I always did my homework at night, I had run a few steps, stopped for a while, and returned to say that I had found no one in the home. I knew it was a sin, but *Mwalimu* Nzyoka's homework was most important to me. He would cane me if I did not finish it.

So when the prizes of merit were given on the day of closing, mine was withheld. The other pupils collected theirs from the office. When I went for mine, the *Muvea* only showed me the ball.

'You are a bad boy. You do not attend Mass and never say your prayers,' he said. 'I will give you the ball when you attend Mass well.'

I needed the ball. So I attended the Sunday Mass, and even the daily Mass during the holiday, in the hope that I would get that ball. But each time, Father Magill would tell me to attend more Masses. As days passed I learned that I was out of favour with him, so kept out of his way.

Two other incidents in Intermediate School stand out vividly in my memory. One day when the bell was rung for the six o'clock Angelus prayer, it seemed that everyone wanted to lead. There was some giggling before the prayer was properly said by the class prefect. After the prayer, one Standard Eight bully, nicknamed Somo, strolled past our classroom. He was probably going home or to the latrines. In a short time he flashed back and entered his classroom. We could guess the reason for his apparent haste. The *Muvea*, Father Magill, was around. We saw him hurry into the bully's classroom and come out holding

Somo firmly by the hand. The two went into Father Magill's office. What went on inside we could only guess. Wooden articles thudded on the floor; we could hear the cupboard or the table being dragged here and there; then only silence.

After a few moments, Somo shot out of the office at top speed, holding his apparently unbuttoned shorts with his left hand. Following him was Father Magill with a cane, his long hair swinging left and right with the motion of the head. We stood and watched the chase through the large spaces in the walls. For about a hundred yards the *Muvea* chased Somo on a clear field. Then they entered the maize field. For about a quarter of a mile, we could trace their positions from the wriggling of the maize tops and the continuous faint cloud of pollen. The bell rang and we rushed for home. On the whole way there was nothing talked of but the chase. For the first time in our history we had seen a European running. It was wonderful to us, but awful for Somo. He had been chased, never to be allowed back to the school. When his father came to plead with the *Muvea*, in spite of the fact that he used the term *Bwana* every few words, Father Magill refused to readmit Somo. This baffled the African *Mwalimu* whom everyone had been calling Headmaster.

The second incident I remember in vivid detail occurred the following year. A big church was being built near the Intermediate School. The construction men were Indians from the city of Nairobi. Every morning Father Magill would come into the school and interrupt the lessons. '*Mwalimu*,' he would say, 'I want these boys to come and help break stones for the concrete. We want to finish building the House of God.' No *Mwalimu* would dare resist. After all, he could be 'sacked' at any moment.

One day our class was interrupted in this manner. The arithmetic lesson was stopped and the period became one of breaking up stones for all of us. *Mwalimu* Munyaka became overseer, and for a whole morning we smashed stones which should have been broken by the construction company. The Indian who was shaping stones nearest us very soon got some of us to order about. He even ordered *Mwalimu* Munyaka, automatically assuming authority by virtue of his being an Indian. After all an Indian was an Asian and an Asian was second to a European and hence above an African. Terrible days, weren't they?

Before we left, we saw the Indian go to the Fathers' house to

make some accusations, we guessed. Then Father Magill came
and said that since we had broken very few stones up to this
time, we would be coming back again in the afternoon. This
annoyed us and *Mwalimu* Munyaka complained.

'Do these people think we are here at this school to build
churches?' he asked, but only of himself.

In the afternoon we went back and broke stones till four,
wasting a whole day's learning. All the classes did the same,
which must have done much to precipitate the clash that came
later, built on strong racial feelings.

It came about one day as we played in the school field during
lunchtime, knowing very well that the two White Fathers were
away. During the game one boy kicked the ball so hard that
it flew far, and bounced right into the centre of a seated group
of Indians. One Indian picked up the ball but held on to it,
and for some time none of us knew how to go about recovering
it. Finally, one small boy decided to go and take the ball at all
costs. He started walking bravely toward the Indians along the
wall of the growing church. When he was directly under one
Indian who was still working on the platform, the group that
had kept our ball shouted something crude in their language.
The Indian on the platform looked below and let fall a *karai*
containing some cement. This missed the boy by only a few
feet. The boy, rushing off in fright at the thud, stumbled and
fell just before reaching the group of Indians. One of them hit
him on the back with the ball he had had in mind to collect.
The Indians laughed at this, but for a short moment only.

A war of stones had started on the other side of the building.
An Indian whom we had nicknamed Kanzi as he resembled a
local Indian, had struck a bully with the large seed of a mango.
The boy retaliated by stoning the Indian. The other boys joined
in, and flying missiles rattled against the half-built wall. Kanzi
tried to defend himself by throwing stones back. But what
could he do against a mob of angered boys?

The battle spread to our side of the building, and it was
'Stone the Indian!' 'Hit the Indian!' 'Kill Gandhi!' from every
mouth. Stones flew fast, each hitting an Indian or the wall.
One or two of the Indians attempted to hit back but then gave
up, running away toward their house. As they did this the
stones were smashing against their backs from the roaring un-
controllable mob of boys. The Indian who had been on the
construction platform was most unfortunate. He shrieked for

help as stones whizzed past him, some of them hitting their mark on his back, legs, and hands. He clambered down a post under a volley of missiles. As he prepared to run, one stone struck his face. The poor fellow fell down and the blood dribbled out. This stopped the stoning, and completely arrested and mastered the mob. Everyone looked and then rushed to disappear round the buildings and into the maize fields. No one wanted to be associated with the terrible incident.

'I think that one died,' said one boy as we ran.

'So what? Even if he dies, who cares?' spoke another. 'This is not India. After all, one of them started it. What if the black boy had died?'

The story spread like wildfire. Those boys who had gone home to have their meals came back with the exciting news of how everybody there was happy about the episode. The Indians were a constant threat to the lives of the labourers. They frequently dropped a stone or a *karai*, or even a hammer, when a black labourer happened to be below. Now when the labourers returned for the afternoon work, they said we were men and had done a fine job. The White Fathers appeared to have heard about the riot when they arrived. Their car sped right to the front of their house, a very unusual action.

From the maize fields, we saw two Indians run to the Fathers' house. After a short time they came towards the school with Father Magill leading. We all knew things would be getting tough soon. *Mwalimu* Njuguna rushed to the place where the school bell stood in silence, and he rang it for a prolonged period. Boys emerged from the classrooms and other hide-outs and assembled in the quadrangle stretching out in front of the classrooms. Everyone knew that the Headmaster had something to say. Otherwise he would not have sent *Mwalimu* Njuguna to ring the bell. I followed my friends to the compound from the direction of the latrines. *Mwalimu* Njuguna was in command. He appeared very much upset.

'Today you will feel it for stoning the Indians,' he said to us. 'Don't you know the *serikali* is powerful and could send the police here . . . and all of us could be beaten, just as they are being dealt with in Kiambu? We don't want Mau Mau boys over here. Remember the white man is great. Don't you see him fly across the blue skies?'

Perhaps you should know that *Mwalimu* Njuguna was a Loyalist, who had managed to take refuge in our area. He had come from Kiambu and spoke often of the horrors the Mau Mau were committing among his people.

Father Magill came to the scene. He was followed by the two Indians and all the teachers. Father Magill surveyed all of us and said nothing. His face was red with rage, his hair rough and appearing to shake as he spoke in low tones to the Headmaster. Then he left. What made him give up his usual air of superiority on this occasion remained a puzzle to all of us. Every time there was an assembly, whether a formal or an impromptu one, it was he who became boss. But now he was clearly refusing to take over the leadership. There was room for us all to guess that, as a European, Father Magill did not want the Asians to associate him with our unruly misbehaviour. He always did avoid parents who accused any of the pupils of bad conduct outside the school, telling them to go to the *Mwalimu*.

So it was the Headmaster, *Mwalimu* Nzyoka, who began, 'I am about to burst in anger to hear that you boys have stoned the Indians. What good are we doing, teaching you every day that Jesus said, "If anyone strikes your left cheek, give him your right," when here you stone the Indians because one boy was struck with the seed of a mango? Don't you see that these Indians are building the House of God and God saw you stone them? I want everyone who threw a stone to take four steps forward!' And he finished with 'God is seeing you!'

A few believed in the words of the Headmaster and took the four steps forward. These were asked to move to the corner of the quadrangle.

'Are those all?' the Headmaster asked one Indian.

'No,' replied Kanzi.

'How many did you see?'

'*Ote napiga jiwe*,' said Kanzi. 'All threw stones.'

The judgement was then simple. All were guilty but some were more guilty than others. These were the ones who had volunteered to confess their crime by moving four steps forward. Some of them had thrown but a few stones, while many of those who held back had done a more thorough job. One boy who had used a catapult made from rubber strips, and had never missed a single shot, was among those who did not confess. The group of boys that confessed were given six hard sticks each right in front of us, and then joined us to partake in the general punishment. We were all forced to kneel down and hold our hands over our heads for a very long time. In fact, the

whole afternoon went in punishment. Instead of playing football
we were made to run round the field many times. When we
were released at six, we were told never to repeat the incident.

But the seeds of hatred for the Indians shot roots quickly.
Everything that belonged to Indians would be pillaged whenever
an opportunity arose. Bottles and looking-glasses were smashed
when they left their house open. Their lorry was stoned, this
on purely individual or small-group initiative.

At last, when the building of the big Church was completed
and the house of God furnished to suit an African user, everyone
who supported Catholicism in the neighbourhood had something
of which to boast. We were proud to have such a huge magni-
ficent building which, in the shape of a cross, symbolized the
glory of Christ. We knew that the Protestants, the African
Brothers and the Salvation Army together could never put up
such a building, no matter how many years they would save.
The building must have converted a few Protestants for some
of them, hitherto anti-*Muveas*, joined in the Sunday Mass.
The children said the prayers louder than ever, probably because
they were entertained by the musical echoes produced at the
corners of the huge cross. When the *Muvea* gave a sermon
before the well situated altar, and there was silence among the
gathering, it was as if God did indeed speak.

'It is on this day that the Word of God will enter the mind
of everyone,' remarked an old woman after the Mass. 'This new
Church is truly a House of God!'

But to some teenagers who had gone astray in life, the new
Church was nothing more than a huge social club. One group
of them brought a guitar and started playing outside as the night
Mass for Christmas was under way. Their singing star seemed to
be telling the *Muvea* to hurry the Mass and release the girls so
that they could go for a dance before morning. Some came into
the Church while still the worse for drink and vomited. Others
smoked at the gates of the Church. This evidently shocked
the Protestants who had turned up for the night Mass, probably
out of curiosity. Some talked about it long afterwards.

7.

Some Lessons in Human Relations

When the time came to go to Secondary School and I was among the fortunate ones, joy ran all through my blood. The Secondary School to which I had been admitted was one of the oldest Mission Stations in Kenya, and its buildings were pretty well worn. The school was situated in a lonely spot remote from any town; to most of our parents, therefore, this was the best possible environment for learning. There was the belief among them that the town always 'spoiled' the secondary school pupils.

The school, when I arrived, was made up of four Irish Fathers, seven African teachers, and about two hundred and fifty pupils in the Intermediate and High School classes. The High School section was headed by a priest whom most of us considered a good fellow. Rather reserved in speech, he had a good sense of justice so far as the school itself was concerned. But this priest wanted nobody to talk politics any time anywhere. One day he threatened to punish my friend Beni if Beni's brother continued to post *The Kenya Comment* to him. This we considered unjust. We felt that *The Kenya Comment* brought politics, in which so many of us were interested at that age, into the open in a frank and honest way.

But it was another Father, nicknamed by us boys 'The Lion' or *Simba*, who was the principal spring of terror in our High School. This Irish priest, according to the school constitution, was the Dean of the Faculty of Studies, charged with responsibility for supervising studies, for issuing text-books and exercise books, and for cyclostyling examination papers. Certainly he went beyond the borders of his Faculty, usurping the duties of the Dean of Discipline, and causing dread everywhere in the compound. Baldness was eating away at the Lion's hair at a steady rate. The space left by a knocked-out tooth in his lower jaw gave rise to all sorts of stories. One was that he had been hit with a piece of firewood by a former cook. His clenched hands could swing terrific blows as he turned the classroom into a boxing ring, freezing with fear all the helpless pupils watching.

The other priests and the lay members of staff were a source of only minor disturbance to us. The actual Dean of Discipline,

Father O'Reilly, who was also the Welfare Officer, was shy and cowardly. He always threatened not to box but to report to the Headmaster. His philosophy of discipline was maintained only within the boundaries of the compound or when some other member of staff was in sight. But more of Father O'Reilly later on. Mr. Karanja, a lay African teacher, could at times blast pupils by both words and blows. He was more feared than the other African teachers but less respected. He always boasted of his stay, though of brief duration, at a University College. Whenever a pupil made a mistake, Mr. Karanja would be tempted to terminate the lesson and relapse into telling the class about life in the college. This, coupled with his first introduction as a new teacher, did much to make pupils talk about him behind his back.

I remember that introduction very well. We had been expecting this new master, having been without a teacher for almost a term. So when the door opened we stood up in all eagerness to meet him.

'Sit down,' the new teacher said, closing the door behind him. Then surveying the class with a critical eye, he dropped his books on the table. This stirred up some chalk dust.

'Who is the monitor here?'

'I am, Sir.'

'That table must be properly dusted before I come in. Understand that, you boy?'

'Yes, Sir.'

The stranger stroked his jacket backwards so stylishly and, bending forward slightly, stood with arms akimbo, his posture more characteristic of a European *Bwana* than of an African.

'Young boys,' he started, after a small fit of coughing, 'you are really very fortunate. I have been commissioned by the Government to come and give you a certain stock of knowledge. You are lucky indeed to be taught by a Graduate. You should always remember that.'

When the bell rang, prayers were said quickly, with some suppressed giggling. Once outside, we would all pose akimbo, reminding one another that we were lucky to have a Graduate as a teacher. When the same master introduced the phrase, 'box physically *and* scientifically', it remained on the tongues of all of us for long. Mr. Karanja's way of talking, walking, and dressing revealed that he considered himself a Black European. Quite a few of the boys chose him as a symbol of what they would be when they left Secondary School.

Another type of African teacher was Mr. Nzomo. The majority rendered him respect simply because the Head of the school demanded it of us. Mr. Nzomo hardly spoke to anyone outside the classroom. He was cruel, too. But we all agreed that he knew his stuff and also knew how to present it. Within the four walls of the classroom we liked him, in spite of the fact that he always brought in two sticks. One was used for striking at close range. The second was for hitting some boy seated at the back of the classroom, otherwise unreachable before the master's anger would cool down. Mr. Nzomo's canings in the classroom, however, were normally forgotten almost as soon as they were given, so absorbed were we in the lessons he taught us.

If any member of the Secondary School staff had a tough time with the boys, it was Father O'Reilly, the Dean of Discipline earlier mentioned. Father O'Reilly had to enforce strict discipline round the clock. This would start with waking up at 6.25 a.m. Then would come in turn Holy Mass, breakfast, classes, lunch, Prep Study, Manual Work, Games, washing at the river, the Rosary or Benediction, supper, studies, and finally sleep. Father O'Reilly had to use a stick to push the boys round and teach us to observe punctuality. He would suddenly turn up in a dormitory as we were dressing to give the order, 'Out now. Quick!' Or he would be seen standing somewhere, exposed to full view, so that everyone would do what he was supposed to do. It was felt among the staff that to make a boy do anything, whether cutting grass, eating fast, playing or any other school activity, someone from the staff had to be around to watch him. This we strongly resented, fighting back silently, which frequently made matters worse.

After a series of explosive escapades by the older boys, I remember, Father O'Reilly would roam about the compound at nights, his spotlight in his left hand and a cane at the ready in his right. He would intercept those going out to the latrines, perhaps to smoke or to relieve themselves. Of course, no one would dare to hold conversation with Father O'Reilly at these odd times. Usually we would dash back into the dormitories or linger about inside the latrines, sometimes for hours on end, until we were sure that danger was no longer at hand. The latrines were the smoking cubicles. It was not unusual to see five, six or more boys squeezing themselves into a latrine to share a piece of cigarette.

Because of the strained relations, some sort of commotion

could be expected at almost any time outside the classrooms. Several boys would be dashing round the corner of a building to dodge a passing member of staff. This might happen when we did not feel like going for Manual Labour or Games, or because we were late for something—study or meals or prayers, perhaps. Still, with all our alertness, for the priests in particular, we used to take time off and talk freely among ourselves during break, or when we would go for the walk by the river. This walk was obligatory every Sunday afternoon. The exact course of the walk was not defined, provided it was along the river, certainly not in any direction where there was a possibility of meeting girls. There was a generally-sensed feeling among us that one of the Fathers was watching through his binoculars. Indeed, there was no trust anywhere in the school, either between staff and students, or between black and white. Everything we did was forced and closely supervised. And this, at our self-conscious late adolescent stage, we strongly and increasingly resisted.

Nonetheless, only a few boys dared take the forbidden paths on these Sunday afternoon 'strolls'. The majority of us stuck to the river banks, swam, basked on the rocks, indulged in all sorts of manly or boyish talk. Some one would begin a topic, perhaps a sensible one, the others joining in to give their views. Then slowly but inevitably the talk would move around to sex, girls, and the priests. The two or three occasions when we did meet girls gave us food for talk and secret hope from each time forwards. I remember one Sunday afternoon in particular. We were basking on the rocks after swimming, with William on the air describing the 'thing' of Petro as extraordinarily long.

'Petro, I think if I were a ship's Captain and you my First Mate,' he said, with his usual mocking laughter, 'I would like you much.'

'But why?' Petro asked, not knowing what was coming.

'You see, and all must see,' answered William. 'Izekiel, don't you think Petro's thing could substitute for an anchor in a rough sea?'

The group laughed loudly. Some rolled off the rocks into the water, quite unable to control themselves.

'You don't know that I am liked by women?' Petro spoke in self-defence. 'I really stir them. If you want me to prove it, go fetch me a woman right now.'

It was such coincidence. As Petro finished speaking, and William was about to criticize his morphology further, four girls emerged, nude, from behind the thicket of reeds, just a few yards below us. They were cooling their bodies in the water and, to begin with, were quite unaware of our presence. Taken by surprise, the boys reacted in a confused, almost brainless manner; at first struck dumb and immobile as they watched. Then William and Izekiel showed their excitement by gesturing wildly to the girls. Petro could only shout, 'Ala-Ala Ala!' and Yohana, 'Here are girls, you! It is true!' Down below, the girls swam about as if to torment us helpless creatures. But it was only a matter of moments before, seeing and hearing us, they too showed their surprise and confusion. With shrieks of embarrassment, and probably pleasure, they quickly scrambled out of view behind the reeds. We waited for their return in vain, some of us standing hopefully on the ledge, some lying on our stomachs, eyes glued to the reeds below. Slowly we began to dress, trying to regain our reason. Some of the boys forgot to put on their vests. And on the homeward walk, I remember, we discovered that Stefano had put his shirt on inside-out. By the time we reached the school, the roll-call was over. We could not believe that the big bell had twice been tolled, none of us having heard it. Most of the boys continued to be restless during study and, later, at dinner. Our rare encounter made news for many many days.

Indeed it used to happen at the school that the very appearance of girls would cause much disturbance. On Sunday mornings we would rush out of the classrooms when the bell rang for break, just to look at the girls streaming to or from the Church. When one of the Fathers realized what we were doing, the Sunday morning study time-table was scrapped. A new one was made, with each of the two breaks coming while Mass was in progress. This did not help much. Whenever one boy would stand up to look outside, a whole classs would shoot up to watch the girls passing by. What satisfaction we got from just seeing girls, the Devil only knew. But whenever a whisper went round that there was a woman in the compound, we would all endeavour to see her at almost any cost. Just see, and then talk about it long afterwards.

Our distorted brand of sex education had started long before this, of course, in the last years of our Intermediate School. From the beginning of our climb up the adolescent ladder, I remember, with the girls appearing to shoot up so much faster than we did, the Fathers had taught us that interest in the opposite sex was evil and contrary to God's will. Still we couldn't help noticing that breasts, feminine looks, perfumed soap, and hair oils were characteristic of the older girls. The big boys had talked of meeting the big girls, but the small ones of us had not understood what they meant. Some of the boys had exchanged letters with the girls, too, which letters, whenever they fell into the hands of the Fathers or of the Sisters at the girls' school, had led to severe canings or even expulsion for both. Any sort of association between the Intermediate School boys and the girls had been strictly prohibited. The Fathers, then as now, had always told us that the mixed company of boys and girls inevitably led to sinning. Any boy found following the girls home, had always been punished by the *Muvea*, while the girls, even though innocent of unbecoming intentions, had been caned by their Sister Headmistress. The girls normally left for home earlier by half an hour than the boys. They had always run straight home in case the Church elders, seeing them slow down, might report them to the Headmistress. Then when the boys, having left the school later, would gain on the girls, we would go rushing past them, lest some Father might be watching behind or ahead of us. We had learned that spies could be anywhere, even at our sides. As I think about it now, it was all such poor sex education, at the very time when the meaning of sex ought to have been taught kindly and properly to the boys and girls.

At the Secondary School, these several years later, the same rigid rules were also laid down, though perhaps because we were older now their enforcement by the staff of the school appeared the more difficult.

'Why don't these white people allow us to mingle with the girls on Sundays?' asked a class prefect one day. 'Then I think we would get used to girls, and stop striving to see them every time they pass by. After all, the white men allow women to come into their houses.'

'So you don't know?' William put in. 'One priest here told us he could never picture an African boy being with a girl and not sinning. I don't know when they will stop attributing bad things to the black skin.' William lowered his voice, as some leather soles milled the gravel outside the classroom. Quickly we picked up our books and shammed reading. Any Father could use this kind of talk as an excuse for severe caning. If asked, 'Why were you talking in the classroom?' even though it was time for break, we would have no defence. The conversation would be resumed, however, once the sound of crushing gravel faded away.

'You know, there is basically no difference between a white priest, a settler, a D.O., or a Police Inspector,' the same leader among us continued. 'They are all Europeans, and crossed the same ocean when coming here. Don't you see how these priests discriminate against any African visitor who comes with a European? He is never allowed to enter their houses. Don't you all see how they refuse to give responsibilities to the African teachers? If you quarrel with the African masters, you are punished. But quarrel with one of the Whites, and you are sent away from the school.'

'If this School were near a big town,' pondered Petro, 'it would be of interest to see how these priests would treat the European boys who came to play against us. I think the Lion would surely join the white boys. I can just hear him shout, "Hey Roy! Roy, don't let that ball pass! Don't be defeated by the sons of your labourers. Smash the chap and go on! Keep your status high everywhere!" I wish white boys *would* come to our school one day. I feel I would thrash one to bits!' And Petro made a jump towards the blackboard in demonstration of how he could hit a white boy.

8.

Rounding Out the Learning

Legally there was only one actual 'head' of the staff of the Secondary School. This was the Headmaster. However, as time went on, there crept in a number of others quite unlawfully. Lion, for example, would frequently pose as the Headmaster, in spite of the fact that he was only in charge of the Book Store. Grogan, the Religious Head of the centre, could order the time-keeper to ring the bell to summon boys for singing in the Chapel. Mr. Karanja talked as if he were the boss, but only when outside the school compound. Parents would come to the school and ask for Mr. Karanja, the Headmaster. Father Ignatius, an old retired gentleman who at times behaved as though he was turning back to childhood, often talked with as much despotic authority as did the Headmaster.

One day, for example, Ignatius met some of us boys at the school field. We were not supposed to be there at the time. Father Ignatius knew this, and made use of it to boss us.

'You boys! Come here!' he ordered.

We went there, standing at attention to wait for the white man to finish the prayer which our presence had interrupted.

'Now say, "I am a foolish boy or a stupid monkey because I have broken a school rule!"' Father Ignatius commanded.

'You are a foolish boy or a stupid monkey because you have broken a school rule,' one boy said.

'You foolish boy!' Ignatius roared. 'Don't you know that I can expel you from the school for this? You are going away tomorrow. Do you understand? I don't want to see you here.'

Oh dear, if a Mission man who did not even know the order of the classrooms could threaten to expel one, who was the real Head? Things sifted themselves out in time, though. The Head was left alone while the false heads dropped out whenever trouble appeared on the horizon. Thus the boys were taught one important thing. When there are no difficulties, everyone wants to be responsible. When things seem to be headed for the worse, nobody cares to be associated with the problem.

Those who had posed as the Head, it so happened, were more than ready to drop the role when two strikes by the students seemed to threaten. One morning the boys came from the Mass, carrying sugar in cocoa tins as they strolled to the dining hall. They lined up and kept silent, as was the rule. The boys who were to serve at table promptly went in and poured porridge on to the plates, then came out shaking their heads. The Head Prefect gave the signal to enter the dining hall. The breakfast bell was tinkled by the Second Prefect-in-Command and, after a few moments' silence, the Head Prefect said the Grace.

'Amen, Amen, A-A-men!' chorused the boys as they opened their cocoa tins of sugar. Some did in fact put sugar into the porridge, stirring it in preparation for taking. Then whispers of 'larvae, larvae in the porridge!' flowed from table to table. Instead of taking the porridge, all the boys started stirring, only to look for larvae. Every table was able to pick out at least some larvae from the porridge.

'That, that's it!' one boy said, and then another. 'I cannot eat it myself.'

Whoever gave the command, Heaven or Hell only knows. But to a man, the boys walked out in protest, to sit or stand outside the dining hall. The time allotted for breakfast was usually short, a quarter of an hour at most. The regulator ran to ring the bell for class. But no one bothered to go to the classrooms. A food strike was on, meaning a strike against other things, too.

Now the Lion, Mr. Nzomo, and other members of staff all appeared in front of their classrooms, then disappeared without coming anywhere near the milling crowd of boys. Ignatius appeared on the avenue but, after a short distance, returned to the Priests' House. Karanja passed by and asked what was wrong but, getting no reply, went his way. The time when no teacher wanted to be Headmaster had arrived.

When the actual Headmaster came to talk to the striking boys, he met with a stone wall at first. To start with, he ordered the boys to go into the dining hall and eat. This they would not do. The boys had been eating weevils for a long time. They were not now going to put up with having to consume larvae. The Headmaster called the prefects and questioned them in the presence of the boys.

'Why didn't one of you come to report to me?' he asked.

No reply from the prefects. They did not want to eat larvae with porridge either. It was when the Headmaster entered the kitchen that he learned why the boys were on strike.

'There are some insects, *Bwana*,' one of the cooks said loudly.

'*Hapana,* no! It cannot be! All this food cannot be wasted!,' boomed the Headmaster.

Coming out of the kitchen he once more ordered the boys to enter the dining hall and eat. No one said a word. The boys in front tried to withdraw to the rear, in case anyone was called upon to enter the dining hall first. The Headmaster began to tremble, either in anger or fright, as the boys defied his orders. His face reddened as his confusion grew. Then after some minutes, he surrendered to the boys.

'Right! You will have the bananas intended for lunch.' Then looking at his watch, he thundered. 'Remember, everyone must be punctual for the 9.30 class!' As he left, the Headmaster took with him two cooks, who brought back bananas which the prefects distributed. After a short time the boys relaxed and went to the classrooms, the mood of the strike still in them.

Lunch time came, the meal this time being a mixture of maize, beans, and black weevils. This was taken as usual. No one objected. The weevils could be removed to a separate plate, that was all. It was only the larvae—ah! ah!—that no one could eat.

The striking spirit lingered throughout the day. In the evening it was stiff porridge and beef for supper. The Headmaster had ignored, or overlooked, the fact that the flour that had sparked off the strike was the same, whether used for porridge or for *ugali*. He came in person to see that the boys ate the awful meal. The parading in front of the dining hall went on as usual. There were some murmurings at the back of the line, in spite of the Headmaster's command to observe silence. When the servers had finished their job inside, the Headmaster indicated to the boys to enter the dining hall. The miserable boys obeyed.

'Say the Grace,' ordered the School Head.

'In the name . . .' started the prefect, but no one seemed to follow, '. . . of the Father and of the Son and of the Holy Ghost, Amen!' As the prefect finished, the boys mumbled 'Amen,' some saying it very late if at all.

We could see the Headmaster marching to and fro outside the dining hall, reading his evening prayers. But who under the sky could read in the falling darkness? The dim light outside was surely not enough. Nevertheless, the white man seemed to be reading with ease. We all knew he was not reading, but only watching for possible trouble.

'I am *not* going to feed on crushed larvae,' declared Izekiel.

'Not me. Perhaps my ghost, but not me. At home we don't have to eat larvae—larvae—larvae!'

'Take the boiled beef and you will be all right, chap,' William said. 'Why don't we do it in the manner Jesus did? We read in the Bible that He went without bread for forty days and forty nights.'

All around the dining hall murmurings were pouring out. Curses and abuses went to all the White priests. Even to the very innocent ones like Ignatius, who was never in any way concerned with food affairs. He had, however, called the boys 'monkeys' at times.

The murmurings stopped at once when the Headmaster entered one end of the dining hall.

'Why are you not eating?' he asked of a small junior pupil. Then picking up a lump of stiff porridge, the Headmaster ate it to show that it was not so bad after all.

'Father, I—I—I—I have consti-constipation,' muttered the boy in utter confusion.

'Nonsense! And since when have you had that?'

By this time many boys had their spoons held ready, but only in pretence. No one wanted to be asked why he did not eat. The pretence convinced the Headmaster that he had after all succeeded in making us eat. As soon as he stepped out, the prefect rang the bell. And after saying Grace, the embittered boys walked out, leaving their meal untouched.

The situation seemed slowly to get out of control. By the following midday, it seemed as if anything could happen, even rioting. Students were talking of a total strike. It was the Head Prefect, who was always abused and lowered in the presence of the boys by staff-members like Lion and O'Reilly, who saved the school from what might have turned into the explosion of the year. Secretly approaching the bewildered Headmaster, the prefect informed him that the boys would rather have a mixture of maize and beans for breakfast than the porridge with larvae. This was agreed to, and worked wonders for about a week. It meant that breakfast was the same as lunch, and lunch equal to supper, always of maize and beans. But at least it was better. Chaos was thus averted, only to appear a few weeks later in another form.

It happened that owing to a shortage of Science teachers, one class was denied any Science whatever in their course. Now who could refuse Science to boys who had just joined the

High School to read Science, whether it meant General Science, Physics, Chemistry, or Biology, and not expect trouble? Science meant learning how to make H_2O, or knowing why an aeroplane flies. It was an important step towards becoming a doctor or an engineer. Indeed, which boy could be said to be 'learned' if he never had science? This was a problem that had been bothering the Form One B Stream class for several months. (The A Stream was having Science.)

One day the whole class sent a letter to the Headmaster, requesting that they be taught Science along with the A Stream. The Headmaster ignored the letter, not bothering to answer. The boys agreed that he might have been justified in not corresponding with his juniors. They sent in another request, getting the same rebuff. A third one met a similar fate. After some days, their classmates in A Stream were experiencing a most interesting experiment, the formation of H_2O in the Laboratory. The B Stream could stand it no longer. The whole class, going quite crazy, one might say, sparked off a real mania for Science.

It happened during the Headmaster's period, the first period in the morning, which was always Religion. When the Headmaster came into the classroom ten minutes late as usual, he found that the class was outside. On the door was a huge placard reading, 'No Science, No School!' Another one read, 'Fees We Pay Equally—Learn Equally We Must.' There was no doubt of it now. This was open rebellion.

'Go into the classroom at once,' shouted the Headmaster, dropping his Catechism and the small Gospel of St. Mark, perhaps in confusion.

Startled, the rebels moved further away from the classroom. They were determined to have no school if there was no Science. The Headmaster followed, the rebels withdrawing backwards as he advanced. When the Headmaster stopped, the rebels stopped too. There was a short pause as they eyed one another in anger.

'You go back to the classroom,' the Father ordered, 'or else you will all go home.'

'Not unless we learn Science!' one boy spoke firmly from the midst of the forty of them.

'Right!' the Headmaster cried in return. 'You come to my office at once. Get your caution money and then you go! Leave School and never come back, unless you have a written statement from either a parent or a guardian that he wants you to return.'

That was the end of the *shauri*. The boys took their caution money back, with Father O'Reilly closely on guard to see that they did not snatch away school property.

Once outside the school compound, the rebels held a tactics council. They decided to stop at nothing. News came back to the rest of the school that their next move was to travel some forty miles, to seek the help of the District Councillors and the District Education Officer. If that failed, they had assured us, the journey would end up in Nairobi, where they would see the members of the Legislative Council for the area. All of us unaffected boys sympathized with them, and of course wished them every success. But none came. The story went that the District Councillors were frozen with fear at discussing anything with anyone who had disobeyed a European. Those were bad days indeed, when an African was totally brain-washed into obeying a white man, right or wrong. When the rebels knocked at the door of the Education Officer, he simply ordered them out. 'Go back and obey first,' was all he would say. When they got hold of the petty politicians, the M.L.C.s, they were promised that the imperialistic, colonial-minded priest would be harshly dealt with. But this was inside. Outside the Office, nothing whatever was done. So the poor rebels, defeated and embarrassed, had to turn to their parents for letters stating that they should be taken back into the school. They came back, and learned no Science. A few were expelled, after being accused of being the instigators. The school returned to normal, with silent opposition growing steadily among the boys.

As the end of the year approached, the external examinations began to threaten the weaker half of the senior class. Boys thought the study period from 7.15 to 9.30 in the evenings was not long enough. Several of them started what later came to be known as the 'Night Campaigns.' The boys would wake up shortly after midnight, crawl out of bed, and go quietly to study in some of the old unused houses, the lamps poor and dim. These campaigns soon came to the knowledge of the Headmaster, however, and it did not take him long to condemn them as foolish, destructive to health, and unnecessary. He threatened to expel anyone caught studying after the official hours.

'To think these old chaps could be really so bad after all!' complained a senior student who had had some town upbringing. 'They don't want us to pass the School Certificate. They want us to fail so that we can go to the *shambas* and take care of the coffee belonging to the *Kaburus*.'

One student, who was caught reading by torchlight in bed, was sent away from class for two days and made to cut grass with the labourers. This was a bad reward. The student was only trying to keep to the spirit of the school, which was to read hard when examinations came near. No one wanted to fail an examination. If the Catechism could be crammed and sung, why not the causes of the American War of Independence, or the whole mercantile system, or even the causes of the South African Boer Trek, or the Indian Mutiny? Clear the History paper with flying colours even if one failed in General Science!

The fact that the Dean of Discipline was against reading after the official night-time study period forced the students to find an alternative. They would jump out of bed earlier than the usual 6.25 in the morning and quietly slip away to the classroom. The faint morning light proved a great obstacle to them, to be overcome only by leaning against the classroom wall which faced the eastern horizon. But this practice, too, came to the attention of the Dean of Discipline and was accordingly declared dangerous to health. It was during a usual Saturday morning 10.30 assembly, when the rules for the week were reviewed or declared:

'No one is to leave his bed before the big bell is rung,' shouted Father O'Reilly. 'Of late I have noticed some foolish stupid boys reading before six, with their backs to the cold stone wall! Where have you been, boys? Don't you know this can cause rheumatism? I will be very severe with anyone found doing it again.'

But the desire to prepare for the final examinations was too great for the worried students. Every available minute of the day was put into use. Notebooks appeared everywhere in the compound. In the chapel boys would be cramming the Catechism instead of keeping trail of the daily Mass. It seemed to us total foolishness to learn the Catechism during the normal study time which could be so valuable for Geography or History or other examination subjects. The Catechism no longer had meaning. But one had to know the right answer as printed, for Religion was Subject Number One in this Secondary school. The students knew that the Bishop's Examination would be coming soon. But since it would not contribute even a fraction towards passing the School Certificate Examination, no one cared much about it, actually.

In the line outside the dining hall, pupils would read as they stood in silence before entering for food. Even while eating, the finalists consumed their notes. It was said to be bad manners not to talk to others at table. But who wanted to be well-mannered at the cost of failing the Examination? Some boys went to the extreme of hiding away from Manual Labour, going off to cram in a bushy area nearby. Even on the Sunday walk by the river, some of the boys would take their notebooks along and cram instead of relaxing. Games were avoided. Playtime was used by them to hide somewhere and read. (This was later on referred to as 'Hibernation.') Some boys quite overdid the business, coming late for study or the Evening Rosary. When questioned as to where they had been, they would give no answer.

Days went fast for the Form Fours, and the examination season arrived. When time came to register for the final examinations, a number of us changed our names, more for reasons of tradition than anything else. Each boy was allowed two names each, by which he would be known henceforth. A few new surnames were adopted, causing some slight confusion. Several of us thought of dropping our Christian names, but questions from the priests made some change their minds.

The day before the School Certificate Examinations were to begin, the Headmaster called the candidates together to announce a new freedom he was about to bestow on us.

'I will allow the Form Fours to go out of the compound on the condition they are not sitting for a paper,' he said. 'You can walk, get fresh air, and relax. It is an experiment, understand. Do not fail it.'

The experiment was failed within a day. The candidates went out after the morning papers were over. The afternoon and the following morning were both to be free of papers. This would give candidates enough time, some were thinking, to become sober before having to sit for a paper the next afternoon. It must have been with something like this in mind that eight of the students got for themselves at a local market some of that intoxicating native drink brewed from sugar-cane juice. Only six of the chaps managed to return to the school compound in time, not for the Evening Rosary nor the supper, but for study at 7.15. The other two had taken beyond what their constitutions could accommodate. So when the six boys arrived, they jovially talked of having left Messrs. So-and-So vomiting beside the road, quite helpless. When the two poor chaps reached the school at nine, just three hours late, one of them collapsed on the stairs on the way to the Headmaster's room. It was very uncommon for students to go to the Priests' House unless their business concerned church affairs, but the beer had worked at least one wonder. It had given these two boys courage to go and fetch the Headmaster from the Priests' House. This had never happened before.

'Which *Mzungu* do you wish to talk to?' asked a servant, upon opening the door.

'The short one. Call the shortest of them all.'

The servant headed for the priests' Recreation Room. When he came out, carrying a silver teapot, he brought the message that the short *Mzungu* was coming. It was quite a stretch of time, however, before the Headmaster appeared. Being a *Mzungu*, he was not to be seen easily without an appointment, especially away from the office.

As the Headmaster approached the two students, one was trying to demonstrate to the other how to maintain balance. He had managed to a certain extent. The weaker one was about to give way to a shakiness in the legs.

'We have come to report to you that we are late, Father,' the steadier student said, slightly trembling.

'We have come to report to you that we are late, Father,' mocked the Headmaster. There was a short pause. And then, 'Any devil could come wobbling along to the Fathers' House and give a similar report,' roared the *Mzungu*. 'Of course, I know what made you late. Go away!' He had perhaps imagined all sorts of things, girls as well as beer, and this made him almost crazy. The next morning after breakfast, he summoned the whole class to a meeting and made some announcements.

'Too much freedom is just like too much generosity. There will always be some individuals to abuse it and to spoil things for the whole community. Since I have been in Africa—and this is some twenty-five years now—I have never met a single grateful African. You do this for them and do that. But what you get is, 'We have come to report that we are late,' or 'We did not do what we were told.' I have been too kind ... But as from this moment,' he bellowed, 'no one is to go outside the school compound. I am going to forget that you have been here for four years. The contents of the Leaving Certificates, which will be posted to your respective homes, will depend on your conduct during these remaining days.'

'What does this man really mean?' muttered Yoana.

'How can he decide to ruin a person's character,' Izekiel asked with scorn, 'by writing about what he does in only one week—and that the last week—of a period of four years?'

Then the champion William took over. 'You see, chaps, we are all good. Our characters have been excellent for four years. But these guys you call Fathers, and I have in mind Lion especially, want to get one of us stuck in life by saying he is indisciplinable, irresponsible, et cetera, et cetera. How can they do that when they talk every Sunday about never to do to another what you would not like to have done to you? Do you remember last month when Lion told us we could do better as labour supervisors on farms or road construction? Who will differ with me when I say there are many inequalities in the world, and one of them is clearly between the white and the black?' William spoke with conviction, but ended with a smile that always betrayed his good nature.

'Don't worry, guys. In three days' time I will leave this school, never to come back until the management is black, in skin and in thought. I will be in Nairobi after Christmas to attend the Postal interview. If I go through, and I hope I will, then engineering will be my profession.' It was the imaginative Yoana who was speaking now. 'One day I well may meet Lion on Government Road, and beside me a girl friend. Then I will say to him, "Lion, you used to beat me whenever I looked at a girl at school. Now here I am with my bride-to-be. Look at me, Lion. Did you think I was going to be a bachelor like you? Yo Yo Yo Yo! Shame be upon you!" Next I will light a cigarette, probably a Du Maurier brand, and puff right into his face.'

Girls, as I have said, were always a favourite topic of conversation. Petro, William, and Beni told us they saw nothing wrong in keeping illegal women, so long as the work was going well. Keeping girl friends, they boasted, probably from no experience, was the only means of disciplining sex before proper marriage. Izekiel wanted to marry straight off. Most of the boys thought a car should be Article Number One to acquire when one started working. They argued that their day-to-day experience in the town showed that if a man drove a car, dressed in a black suit, and worked somewhere, he could always find girls. Girls wanted anything that made the sound of a machine, they said, reasoning that if a gentleman could maintain a car that consumed petrol he could easily maintain a wife who fed on food from the *shamba*.

'Anyway, woman, car, job, all must wait for now,' advised Beni. 'Finish the Examinations and Secondary School first. Then we shall go into life headlong.'

Thus it was that the silent opposition, always a dangerous thing, was strong among the final year students at our School. Two days before the closing, this silent opposition to the authorities of the school began to show itself anew. Four, five, even six boys would sit on a bed normally meant for one and crumple it down, thinking that by so doing they were making it bad for the Fathers. In reality, it only caused the juniors' life to be more miserable the following year, since the juniors would be fined for damaging school property, an early item of business for every new year.

On the final night at the school, there were four boys who, claiming to have suffered most at the hands of the Lion, formed a saboteurs' group. They went round in the dead of night trying their hands at anything that could be detached or broken. When the water taps proved unbreakable, they opened them up full force, letting the water flow to waste.

And that was not all. The school was built on a small hill, the eastern side of which was precipitous. An old half-used brick house stood at the top of the cliff, its airy veranda facing the river valley down below. Not many feet below the veranda grew some *Ngoja Kidogos*, plants with vicious hooked thorns which would never release their grip. On the veranda was kept a set of sofas. These were used by the white Fathers as they rested, reading prayers and watching, through their binoculars, the movements of the boys down in the river valley. The Lion, the school's arch-enemy, always sat on one of these sofas and smoked in a leisurely fashion. No wonder, then, that the sofas made an attractive target for our four saboteurs.

It was 3.30 in the morning when, reaching the veranda, the boys sank down onto the sofas.

'Ha ha ha! I am *Simba* himself,' said one, leaning back in smart imitation of the Lion. 'Please give me a cigarette.'

'My Lord God, Creator of Heaven and Earth, what can I do to render real service to *Simba*?' another saboteur asked on his knees.

'You don't pray to God at such a time as this,' said the gang mobilizer, now under the influence of drink for the first time in his life. 'Instead you should pray to Satan and see how much good you pull out. But let's waste no time on such matters,' he warned, taking a match-box from his pocket.

'No no! Let us not set the sofas on fire,' a small but intelligent boy put in. 'The fire will smell and wake up the priests. Let us just throw them over the cliff.'

While this suggestion sank in, the boys sat on the sofas for long, imitating every character on the staff as they talked and laughed together. After about half an hour of this, the real sabotage work began. The sofas were lifted by the four boys, and swung forwards and backwards to gather momentum. Then with One, Two, Three, and *Four*, each of the sofas went rolling over the cliff, breaking to pieces some one hundred yards away. Each of them, that is, but one, which was held fast by the powerful *Ngoja Kidogo* hooks. (It was this, the boys realized helplessly, that would give the clue to the sofas' disappearance.)

'Smash the windows!' one boy shouted, in anti-climax. But this was unanimously agreed to be bad. The small house was used by one of the priests for the morning Mass. In it stood a minute altar and, according to what the gang had learned, action against it would have been blasphemy.

As the saboteurs returned to their respective dormitories, silently and cautiously, they planned to smash the wind-screen of the school's Mission car. This no doubt would have taken place, had they not suddenly seen the flash of a torch. This surprise set them in flight, and saved the school car from damage.

By daylight on that final morning we all gathered for what we knew to be the last roll-call ever for the school's leavers. No credentials were given, the Headmaster promising to send them by post. At seven o'clock we boarded a bus and took off, some to return the following year, others to go into town, in any case a new life for all. But that will be another story.

Glossary

Lijembe

Askaris	the Chief's policemen
Boma	enclosure where cattle are kept
Buhasyo	co-operative efforts
Bujeni	left-over food
Bukhulu	dance involving circumcision rituals
Bushuma	millet porridge
Idiolo and Ikhuya	hockey-type games, with maize-cob used as ball
Ikambi	place of meeting for the mmasitsa
Ing'ombe	guessing game, with object hidden in one hand
Isukudi	a drum-like instrument
Kongolo	game involving envious, dangerous, childless beast
Lihu	a slippery type of vegetable
Luseshe	a siphon used especially for beer-drinking
Luseso	a tough grass
Madili	temporary houses
Manani	wild beasts
Mavuya	special type of soft leaf
Miikho	a wooden piece used for preparing bushuma from maize or millet flour
Mmasitsa	a Sunday social
Mukoye	a wrestling festival for youths
Shamba	garden or cultivated plot
Shihango	roasted meat kept on hand for emergencies
Shiko	area of house used by animals at night
Shilemba	a group game or dance
Shitandawili-ndega	story or riddle-telling period
Tsisimba	sleeping places for youths
Viyumbu	banana ends
Wetee	signal for the start of a mock beer-party session

Apoko

Abiia	shrine to the gods
Abutidda	catapults for shooting stones

Adungu	a musical instrument played by girls
Ceno	a string skirt
Cobo lawala	a spearing game played by boys, using lawala
Gara	little bells
Iwang oo	around the fire
Kwashiorkor	malnutrition disease
Lapidi	a child nurse, frequently a relative or neighbour
Lawala	a willow bent and tied as a ring
Luk	unmarried women
Malakwang	a sour green vegetable
Malaya	prostitutes
Ngala	teasing
Obeno	piece of cloth used for tying the baby on the back
Ododo	educative stories

Nzioki

Ajai	term of exclamation
Hapana	no
Jembes	hoes for digging
Kaburus	Boers
Karai	heavy metal basin
Muvea	Catholic priest
Mwalimu	teacher
Mzungu	European
Pangas	curved knives for cutting grass
Serikali	Government
Shauri	affair
Shenzis	heathens
Toto	houseboy
Ugali	stiff porridge

Printed by *Kenya Litho Ltd.*, P.O. Box 775, Cardiff Road, Nairobi.
Published by *Oxford University Press*, P.O. Box 12532, Nairobi, Kenya.